FALKLANDS/MALVINAS
Whose Crisis?

STDMISXNOBLE

Latin America
Bureau
Research and action on Latin America

First published in Great Britain in 1982 by

Latin America Bureau (Research and Action) Ltd
1 Amwell Street
London EC1R 1UL

Published with the assistance of:

Catholic Institute for International Relations
Methodist World Development Action Fund
Quaker Peace & Service
War on Want

The views expressed however, are those of the authors

Written by Martin Honeywell and Jenny Pearce
Additional research and writing by Simon Barrow, David Fig, Henry Finch,
Patricia Holland and Rafael Runco
Design by Jan Brown Designs
Cover photo by Barry Lewis/Network
Maps by Michael Green
Typeset, printed and bound by the Russell Press Ltd, Nottingham

Contents

Preface

Reports from the South Atlantic that filled the media with stories of Exocet missiles, landings at San Carlos, the battle for Goose Green and the advance on Port Stanley are now rapidly fading memories. Yet the controversy surrounding the events countinues unabated. Was it vitally necessary for Britain to go to war over distant islands that most people had never heard of and from which all but token military defence had been withdrawn? The assumption underlying Britain's military action are now being examined very closely.

Our purpose in publishing this book is to question those underlying assumptions and in so doing challenge the pro-war consensus that was nurtured during the ten-week crisis. We focus specifically on the island's internal economy, on the conflicting British and Argentine claims to sovereignty, on the historical relationship between the two countries, and on the military dictatorship in Argentina since 1976 which received backing from Britain. Apart from a short chronology of events, this book is not about the war itself. Instead we hope it will provide readers with the background information necessary to assess the real issues that were at stake in the South Atlantic.

It is clear that the popular press in Britain played an important role in the process of forming public opinion about the crisis. We have included a short appendix which looks more closely at the implications of that coverage.

For stylistic reasons we have not referred to the islands as the Falklands/Malvinas throughout the text. Where we use one or other of the names independently, we do not imply any judgement on the conflicting claims to the sovereignty of the islands.

Latin America Bureau
July 1982

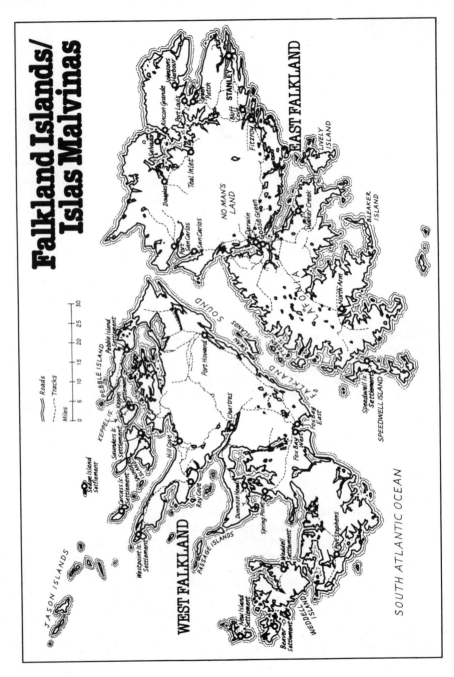

Falkland Islands/Islas Malvinas

The Falklands/Malvinas In Brief

Area	4,700 sq. miles	
Population	Total	1,813 (1980)
	Growth	fall of 24% since 1932
	Urban	60%
Principal towns	Port Stanley	1,050 (1980)
	Goose Green/	
	Darwin	100
The People	Origins	British settlers. Of the present population, 17% were born in Britain and 75% were born on the islands.
	Language	English
	Religion	Church of England
		Roman Catholic
		Non-conformist
Economy	GDP	Total £2,678,000 (1974)
		Per capita £1,477
	Trade	Exports £2,239,000
		Imports £ 805,200
		All exports went to Britain and 82.3% of imports came from Britain in 1974.
	Principal export	Unprocessed wool makes up 99% of exports.

Sources: An Economic Survey of the Falkland Islands (The Shackleton Report)
Economic Intelligence Unit Ltd, London, July 1976; *The Falkland Islands Gazette.*

1 The Island Community

The war in the South Atlantic has thrust the small Falkland Island community into the international spotlight. As a backdrop to the conflict, the islands have been presented as everything from an idyllic pastoral community to a treeless, windswept outcrop. Neither description is very useful. There are however, several important factors that need to be considered if the islands are to be understood. The steady population decline and the inexorable run down of the dominant industry, sheep ranching, are crucial. Also important is the fact that the vast majority of the land is owned by absentee landlords who have steadily decapitalized the islands, that is, withdrawn their farming profits rather than reinvested them in the local economy. And finally, the bureaucratic and undemocratic colonial administration, coupled with the almost feudal control that many of the farming companies exercise over their employees, explain the apathy and despondency that beset the islands.

Situated just 480 miles north-east of Cape Horn, the Falkland Islands were on a busy exploration route for maritime adventurers seeking to round the Horn in the 16th and 17th centuries. It is told that the earliest recorded name for the islands was that given by Captain Hawkins, an Elizabethan corsair. He called them Hawkins Maidenland 'in perpetual memory of her chastity (Queen Elizabeth I) and my endeavours'. The name Falkland Islands is probably an extension of the name Falkland Sound, by which Captain John Strong in 1690 named the narrow stretch of water between East and West Falkland, presumably in honour of Anthony Cary, Third Viscount

Falkland, then a commissioner of the Admiralty. The Spanish name for the islands, Las Islas Malvinas, is a derivation from the French name Les Malouines, recalling the intrepid Breton sailors from St Malo, who fished and sealed in these waters in the early 18th century.

The Falkland Islands consist of two large islands, East and West Falkland, and some 200 smaller islands. Together they have a land area of 4,700 sq. miles, somewhat smaller than Wales. The two main islands are generally hilly, except in Lafonia, the southern half of East Falkland. The hills rise to over 2,000 feet and are generally bare of vegetation. Trees will not grow in the prevailing climate and the natural vegetation on the lower ground is rough grassland comparable to that found in upland Britain. Much of the lowland areas are wet and boggy. The climate shows a narrow temperature range (from 36°F to 49°F), strong winds with frequent gales, and a low but steady rainfall throughout the year. The islands have an abundance of wildlife, geese, penguins, seabirds and seals.

The 1980 census of the islands recorded a population of 1,813 people, of whom 1,360 were born locally (see Table 1, page 127). Of the rest, 360 were born in Britain and had either settled on the islands or were engaged in short term contract work; 30 were Argentinian, operating the fuel depot and air services, and the remainder were immigrants, often farm labourers, from various countries. The overall population has declined by 25 per cent since its peak in 1931. This decline has been more marked among the locally born 'kelpers' (a name which derives from kelp, the local seaweed) than among the expatriate population. The decline is due mainly to young people leaving the islands in search of jobs and a more modern lifestyle. This is especially true of the female population, many of whom marry expatriate workers and leave with them when their contracts expire. This leaves a predominantly male population on the islands. In some age ranges women make up only 39 per cent of the population. The situation is worse in the countryside. In West Falkland in 1972, in the age range 20 to 29, women comprised only 29 per cent of the total population.

The islands' capital Port Stanley is located on the east coast of East Falkland. Nearly 60 per cent of the total population, 1,050 people in 1980, live in the capital. It is the seat of the Falkland Island government, contains various installations of the Falkland Island Company (FIC) such as jetties, offices and warehouses, and contains other elements of the social infrastructure such as the King George Memorial Hospital, the high school, the Upland Goose Hotel, the Colony Club, and 15 to 20 small retail outlets including West Stores, the Falkland Island Company's 'supermarket'. Prior to the war the population of Port Stanley was made up of various distinct groups.

There was a group of expatriate short contract experts (around 50 in number) who staffed the government and various development projects being sponsored from Britain. Then there were the local employees of the government and the Company, the town's only employers. And finally there were settlers from the countryside. These are mainly older people, who having retired from working on the sheep ranches, have had to vacate their tied houses and seek accommodation in the capital.

Outside Port Stanley, in the area referred to as the 'camp' (from the Spanish *campo* meaning countryside) there are about 35 settlements. The largest of these is at Goose Green and neighbouring Darwin which has over 90 inhabitants. The shepherds and farm workers live in tied cottages or communal bunkhouses. Port San Carlos, (where British forces landed on 21 May), is a typical large settlement of around 50 inhabitants. It was described in *The Observer* of 27 May 1982:

Immediately above the jetty is a scattering of wood-framed buildings with corrugated steel walls and roofs; the wool shed surrounded by sheep pens, the diesel oil tank, the bunkhouse for unmarried farmhands, the two storey cookhouse and the peat sheds. Further on you come to houses for families, the engine shed which houses the electrical generator, the long low schoolhouse and a protective structure, made from squares of gorse, for newly shorn sheep without which they would otherwise die of exposure. Then, through a white gate and up a long drive, you reach the 'Big House', the large, Swedish weatherboard home of the farm manager.

The settlements are largely self-sustaining. Each family has its own vegetable garden and domestic animals. The few items that cannot be provided locally — flour, tea, canned goods and sugar — can be bought at the farm store.

Prior to the recent conflict, the islands' main link with the outside world was by way of the weekly flight operated by LADE, the Argentine government's air service. Carrying passengers, mail and general cargo, LADE's short haul aircraft operated a service to Comodoro Rivadavia in southern Argentina. The Port Stanley airstrip was not capable of accommodating intercontinental flights. Since the Falkland Island Company withdrew its monthly sea link with Montevideo in 1971, it has been replaced by a sea link direct to Britain. The Dutch ship *AES*, chartered by the company, makes the five-week trip from Gravesend to Port Stanley four times a year. It carries consumer goods and other supplies on the outward trip and returns with the wool clip. The islands also have radio, telex and telephone communications with the outside world.

Communications within the islands themselves are very difficult. With only six miles of paved roads, and all of that in and around Port Stanley, access to the rural areas by land is restricted to camp tracks.

3

These are only usable by Land Rover, and the 50-mile journey from Port San Carlos to Port Stanley takes 12 to 14 hours. There are approximately 1,000 road vehicles registered in the islands. Most internal passenger transport is carried by the Falkland Island Government Air Service (FIGAS), which, operating two Beaver float planes and an Islander land plane, links all the outlying settlements to Port Stanley. It also operates the flying doctor service. Freight transport to the settlements and collection of the wool clip is carried out by two company managed coasters, the *MV Forrest* and the *MV Monsunen*. They also make occasional trips to Punta Arenas in Chile. All the settlements are linked to Port Stanley by telephone or radio telephone.

The government that sits in Port Stanley has jurisdiction over the Falkland Islands and its dependencies, South Georgia and the South Sandwich Islands, Shag Rocks and Clerke Rocks. All are uninhabited except South Georgia on which there is a British Antarctic Survey Station at King Edward Point. Britain's territorial claims south of latitude 60°S are administered separately under the title of the British Antarctic Territory. The Falkland Island government is run by a Governor appointed by London, assisted by an Executive Council and a Legislative Council. The Executive Council, which could be roughly described as the island's cabinet, is made up of two ex-officio members, two unofficial members appointed by the Governor and two elected members from the Legislative Council. The latter, which meets two or three times a year, consists of the Governor, the Chief Secretary and the Financial Secretary of the islands, together with six elected members. Elections are held every five years: at the 1981 elections a little over 1,050 people were eligible to vote.

The Falkland Island government has been accused of being undemocratic and inefficient. Power rests in the hands of the non-elected Governor who exercises effective control over the Executive Council. Such democracy as did exist merely allowed the local farm managers and land owners some voice in the Legislative Council, a body with little real power. The working class 'kelpers' had no political party and no voice in government. It is interesting to note that one of the first reforms suggested by the British government at the end of the hostilities with Argentina concerned changes to the islands' colonial administration which would give the islanders a greater degree of self-government.

The islands' health service is operated from the King Edward Memorial Hospital in Port Stanley. The three doctors, the dentist and three nursing sisters are all on short-term contracts from Britain. They are assisted by seven locally trained nurses. The hospital is able to deal with most cases but referred serious ones (some 45 in 1981) to Buenos

Aires. The same personnel also operated the flying doctor service and the radio telephone surgery hour. The latter consists of the doctors calling the settlements every morning and advising the farm managers of how to treat minor complaints among their workforce.

Education on the islands is compulsory up to 15 years. Primary education is provided by various local schools or by peripetetic teachers who visit the outlying settlements. The high school in Port Stanley had 85 pupils and served the whole of the Falkland Islands. A school hostel was planned to accommodate pupils from outlying areas. Few pupils achieve 'O' level standard. Those wishing to study 'A' levels have to come to Britain, but the number of those doing so is very small. Most of the teaching staff are on short term contracts from Britain.

Socially the islands were by no means a quiet rural paradise before the conflict altered things so dramatically. The steady decline in population underlines the fundamental problems. The main industry, sheep ranching, is almost exclusively controlled by absentee landlords. There is little chance of local farmworkers ever aspiring to own their own land either on an individual basis or communally, in the form of local cooperatives. Extensive ranching requires few workers, and many young people are obliged to leave to find work. Those who remain have to work as farm labourers under what amount to feudal conditions. They buy all their provisions at the company store, they eat company mutton, they live in company houses and the local farm manager living in the 'Big House' has total control over the settlement. Because of bad communications, many people seldom leave their settlements and many have never visited Port Stanley. This isolation and dependency on the local landowner led to frustration, despondency and inertia.

This situation caused serious social problems. Families are broken up as older children leave the islands to search for work, elderly relatives leave the settlements when they are forced to vacate their company houses at the end of their working lives, and school children must go to live in Port Stanley if they are to receive secondary education. This forced movement of people leads to severe individual distress. For many people, the only outlet for their frustrations is in excessive drinking. The social malaise is also illustrated by the high rate of divorce. Between 1965 and 1974, over 25 per cent of all marriages on the islands ended in divorce, a rate approximately three times higher than in Scotland.

Sheep, sheep and more sheep

The economy of the Falkland Islands is totally dominated by the

5

production of wool for exports. Mainly because of the poor quality of the pastures, the farming is based on extensive sheep ranching and farms of over 100,000 acres are not unusual. Sheep farming has formed the economic basis of the islands since the 1870s. Falklands wool is widely judged as being at the finer end of the quality range. It is noted for its softness, springiness and fibre strength. Despite this, there have been no successful attempts to diversify into other sheep-related products or to process the wool clip into finished products. As with other raw materials, wool has not maintained its value over the years and the local wool industry has been in steady decline since 1919. This decline has been exacerbated by the lack of investment in modern technology and therefore productivity has constantly fallen.

The total wool clip declined steadily throughout the 1960s and early 1970s. It revived somewhat in the mid-seventies before starting to fall once again. The total clip in the 1980/81 season amounted to 4.66 million pounds of wool. However, to obtain that quantity of wool, 593,889 sheep had to be shorn. In the 1963/64 season, 4.81 million pounds of wool were obtained from shearing 573,897 sheep, pointing to the gradual decline in the quality of the pasture available and therefore the quality of the sheep.

The economic uncertainty involved in the production of wool for export is clearly illustrated by the wide price variations that the producers have received for their clip over the years. Port San Carlos has recorded variations in price of over 100 per cent between 1972 and 1980.

Reported wool selling price, Port San Carlos
(in pence/kilo)

1972	1973	1974	1975	1976	1977	1978	1979	1980
57	65	117	56	98	127	115	124	114

Source: Port San Carlos Ltd, *Annual Company Reports.*

With steadily rising production costs this instability in the wool price makes future profitability uncertain and therefore deters investment.

Attempts to diversify the economy have not been successful. This is a natural outcome of the type of economic development being imposed on the islands. The absentee landlords who control the islands measure success solely in terms of the levels of profit which they are able to extract. The resulting decapitalization means that capital is not being accumulated locally. Without such local capital there is no investment in roads, power generation, port facilities and the education necessary to provide a skilled local labour force. Because of these drawbacks, the islands do not attract new industry. Furthermore, reliance on Britain as the major supplier for the islands' needs and as a market for their products places a severe restraint on development. Transport costs for the 8,000-mile journey (as compared to the 400-mile journey to Argentina) make the marketing of local products in Britain uneconomic.

Examples of attempts to diversify the economy are numerous. Most relate to sheep or wool products. Mutton forms a large part of the local diet and in the 1980/81 season, 6,773 sheep were slaughtered for consumption in Port Stanley and 12,805 for the settlements. However, it has not been possible to develop an export trade in mutton. In 1953, the Commonwealth Development Corporation constructed a meat freezing plant at Ajax Bay to prepare mutton for export. It operated for just two years. It was found that the difficulties of transporting the sheep to the plant and the high cost of transport from the Falklands to the final market made the operation unprofitable.

The other major problems concerned the quality of the animals available for slaughter and the regularity of supply. A large proportion of the sheep for slaughter were of low quality and therefore unsuitable for consumption. This is a natural consequence of the extensive farming technique, where the wool clip is maximized by having a very large number of sheep rather than concentrating on a high wool yield per head. This way of farming also affected the regularity of supply, since obviously, sheep would not be sold for slaughter before the shearing was complete. This resulted in a large supply being available at certain times of the year but no supply at other times. Accommodating these irregularities would have meant the provision of extensive cold storage facilities, which, given the islands' poor infrastructure would not have proved viable.

The processing of sheepskins for export represents a minor cottage industry on the islands. Between 1965 to 1974, exports of sheepskins fell in value from £36,600 to £11,400.

No attempts have been made to process the wool clip locally. It is argued that the size of the clip would not be sufficient to maintain a high technology, capital intensive scouring or spinning plant operating for more than a few weeks per year. As this is the only sort of plant which could generate the profits that foreign investors would require, it is obviously an uneconomic proposition for them. They also argue the lack of local skilled labour and the poor local communications would also make the operation very expensive. Given the non-availability of processed wool on the islands, no significant knitting or weaving industry has developed despite the existence of a small local tourist market. The home knitting and weaving that does occur is based on imported wool.

The production of other foodstuffs for local consumption has also declined over the years. During the Second World War, local self-sufficiency in vegetable crops was encouraged by the British government and in 1949 a total of 150 tons of a wide range of vegetables was marketed. However, commercial horticulture has subsequently declined dramatically and substantial quantities of dried and tinned vegetables are now imported. Dairy production has never been carried out on a commercial basis. Most farms provide for their own needs but output per head is low. Consequently, both milk and cheese are imported in large quantities. The consumption of dairy products per head is approximately half that of the UK.

The islands have a small tourist industry, but again lack of local infrastructure, in this case an international airport and hotel facilities, has hindered its development. Three sorts of tourists visit the islands. A small number come each year to observe and study the local wildlife. A second group consists of Argentinians who come to buy electrical consumer goods. Depending on the relative value of the Argentine peso against the pound, such goods can be cheaper on the islands than on the mainland. A third group of tourists are those who visit the islands from passing cruise ships. In 1975, six cruise ships, bringing a total of 6,000 tourists, made brief calls at Port Stanley.

Failure to diversify the economy does not mean that the islands have no economic potential. It is clear that a move away from extensive sheep ranching to more intensive cultivation (producing both for local needs and for export), investing in local infrastructure and a rerouting of the exported profits back into local investment could produce a healthy economy that could support two or three times the current population. However, that will not happen if the present land ownership pattern continues.

In 1974 the service sector of the economy employed 54 per cent of the economically active population. At least half were employed in building and construction and government administration, and a further quarter in transport and distribution. The service sector is completely dominated by two employers, the Falkland Island government and the Falkland Island Company. Their employment policies do little to develop a competent local labour force. In 1976, just over half of the senior civil servants and many others in middle grades were expatriates who received salary supplements over and above their government salaries. These employees were contracted under the Overseas Service Aid Scheme (OSAS) which by definition was not open to applications from islanders. This led to a two-tier employment situation, wage differentials and a considerable 'brain drain' when employees left at the end of their contracts. The low level of local educational standards and the lack of training facilities meant that islanders were consistently unable to compete with expatriate 'experts' for local jobs.

The wages of hourly paid workers were the subject of an annual agreement signed by the General Employees Union, the government and the Falkland Island Company. It applied to all their employees in Port Stanley. The GEU, formed in 1943, is the only union registered on the islands. Its membership is open to all hourly-paid workers both in Port Stanley and in the camp. In 1975 it had 442 members (roughly half of the economically active population) who paid £10 annual membership. According to the wages agreement published in February 1982, the hourly rate for tradesmen amounted to £1.53½, plus extra payments of 15p to 20p per hour for dirty or hazardous work. This gives a weekly wage of a little over £60, which compares unfavourably with the average weekly farm wages in England and Wales of £99.09 (for the year ending March 1982).

Wages in the camp were the subject of agreement with the islands' Sheep Owners Association. In 1975 its membership covered all but one of the islands' farms. Wage negotiations took place annually during July. However, the situation in the camp is more complex than in Port Stanley, because part of the wage is received in kind. Farm labourers in the settlements receive 'free' accommodation, meat, milk and peat, still the main source of fuel. Other consumer goods are available at the farm store and many settlements operate the 'truck' system whereby the workers buy on credit and have the bill deducted from their wages at the end of the week. For many workers, credit at the company store obviates the need to handle money at all as in most settlements there is nowhere else to spend it. So instead of drawing the balance of their wages they would be allowing the company to act as their unofficial banker, accumulating the total balance in its books. In this way they have effectively been making interest-free loans to their employers.

It has been argued that the islands suffer a continual labour shortage, which explains the absence of unemployment and the fact that many people hold various part-time jobs. This assertion must be questioned, however. It is not uncommon for people in small island communities to do several jobs because local demand for any professional service is not sufficiently developed so as to allow many individuals to specialize on a full-time basis. The absence of unemployment is essentially due to the fact that those for whom there is no work leave the islands in search of better prospects. Potential unemployment is therefore exported. While it is true that many jobs on the islands are filled by expatriate workers, this has more to do with the lack of educational and training facilities available to the islanders which would enable them to compete on an equal footing with the overseas 'experts'. So islanders have to leave whilst expatriates are brought in.

In the camp, it is true that staffing levels on the farms have been falling for some time. In 1974, an hourly-paid labour force of 382 people was employed. This had fallen by about 15 per cent by 1980. However, this reduction is more closely related to the overall decline in the profitability of wool production than to a shortage of local labour. It is also suggested that local labourers, who have higher expectations and are more expensive to employ (in terms of housing and education for their families, for example) are being replaced by imported single labourers. As was pointed out in the islands' Legislative Council, the practice of bringing in Chilean labourers to the camp has been going on for many years.

In 1973, the Falkland Islands government employed no less than 73 pensionable officers; its proposed budget for 1981/82 amounted to a little less than £3.5 million, the equivalent of approximately £1,800 per head of population. The budget provided only £40,694 for training and agricultural development, a figure slightly lower than the cost of financing the governor and his household staff. The cost of running the government secretariat, the treasury and the central stores amounted to £190,293. Education, medical services and social welfare accounted for £630,258, less than 17 per cent of the total budget. On the income side, government revenue was highly dependent on the profitability of wool production. The estimated government revenue from taxation on the company's wool profits amounted to 38 per cent of total government revenues in 1975/76.

Export statistics show the extent to which the islands can be described as a 'one-crop economy'. In each of the ten years from 1965 to 1974, unprocessed wool accounted for 99 per cent of total exports (see Table 5, page 129). The total quantity of wool exported remained almost constant over the period but the receipts obtained from its sale varied considerably according to the prevailing wool price.

Wool Exports

	1965	1968	1971	1974
Wool exported (kg)	2,195,900	2,045,600	2,053,900	2,004,700
Value (£)	1,003,900	810,800	651,900	2,225,200

Source: Shackleton Report, 1976.

The only other export that has been sustained throughout the period was dried and salted hides and skins. However, the quality of skins available makes them unattractive for export. The value of such exports has halved over the period.

In 1974 imports amounted to £805,200. As would be expected for a non-diversified, monoculture economy, a large percentage of those imports are of manufactured products. Over 40 per cent of total imports come into this category. What is more surprising is the islands' dependence on imported food and beverages. These represent nearly 40 per cent of total imports and this clearly illustrates the inability of the islands to supply their own food under present conditions. Previous experience has shown that the islands could produce the majority of their food needs if the constraints imposed by absentee landlords were removed.

It is clear from the figures that the islands have a healthy trade surplus. Had the assets employed in the Falklands been owned by local people, this would have given rise to a large inflow of resources into the islands which would have been available for local consumption and development needs. However, this was not the case. The majority of the profits from the sale of the wool clip accrued to the absentee landlords who own most of the farms on the islands. These profits therefore have never found their way back to the local economy.

The slow but steady contraction of the local economy can be seen by the steady fall in the islands' gross domestic product (GDP), that is, the value of all the wages, profits and rents generated by the local economy. When measured at constant 1974 prices, the GDP has fallen from £3,028,200 in 1966 to £2,678,100 in 1974.

Who tends the sheep and who gets the sweater

'The Falkland Islands fit surprisingly well into the familiar economic pattern in Latin America, of reliance on one crop . . . with the resulting monoculture dominated by one big company'.
The Times 2 December 1968.

The islanders are kept in a 'near feudal state of dependency by absentee landlords, under-investment and inadequate government'.
The Times 21 July 1976.

Farm managers exhibit a 'large degree of paternalism, together with a feudalistic attitude that has tended to sap a lot of individual responsibility and initiative'.
The Times 21 July 1976.

There can be little doubt that Britain's sovereign control of the Falkland Islands represents an historical anachronism. When national boundaries were being redrawn in the early nineteenth century at the end of the era of Spanish colonialism, Britain managed to retain a territorial toehold against the flow of history. However, although Britain's colonial control of the islands may be anachronistic, there is no reason to believe that the present island economy is similarly out of step. It represents nearly all the traits of a classic late twentieth century dependent economy, which, were it in continental Latin America, Africa, or Asia we would definitely categorize as underdeveloped. It may not exhibit the same levels of poverty as other underdeveloped countries, but it displays the same dependence on the export of raw materials, the same lack of diversification in the economy, the same dependence on foreign capital (that is, capital entering the islands from outside), the same lack of economic and social infrastructure and the same lack of representative democratic structures. This state of affairs has existed in the Falkland Islands since the late 1920s and early 1930s and serves the interests of certain economic groups associated with the islands.

It is clear that the aspirations of these different economic groups are antagonistic. There are four such groups. Firstly there are the immigrant farm labourers, who seek to maximize earnings during their brief working spells on the islands, and then leave with as much of what they have earned as possible. They are not concerned with the social or economic development of the local economy. The kelpers, the indigenous working class, while also trying to maximise their wages, are in addition concerned with the social and political environment of the islands. Education, housing and other government policies affect their lives and they seek to have some voice in the formulation of those policies. The third group consists of the land-owners who either work their own land or employ local labour to work it, but who themselves live on the islands. They would find many points concerning the overall development of the islands on which to agree with their local labour force. Their aspirations could loosely be defined as 'nationalistic'.

The fourth interest group is that of the absentee landlords. They own the vast majority of the farms on the islands, and most of the economy depends on them. However, their interest in the islands centres around the annual dividend that their landholdings generate. They are by no means a homogeneous group. On the one hand there are individuals and families who, although kelpers by birth, have now left the islands to live abroad. Although they still retain many of the 'nationalistic' aspirations of the resident kelpers, their emotional attachment to the islands slowly breaks down over time. The other end of the scale is represented by Coalite Ltd, the owners of the Falkland Island Company. For the Coalite shareholders, their investment in the Falklands must, by the nature of the economic world in which they live, be judged by its profitability. They judge that extensive monocrop agriculture in a non-diversified economy best serves their interests. (If this was not the case, they would invest in other projects on the islands.) Such an agricultural system does not serve the best interests of the islands' community.

On a political level, the General Employees Union represents the working class kelpers, and to a lesser extent the immigrant labourers, in their wage negotiations. However, the GEU does not play a major political role in other aspects of the islands' life and is not, for example, represented in government institutions. The conflict of interests between the local kelper landowners and the absentee land-owners is reflected within both the local and the British governments. Both governments have to approve the islands' fiscal regulations which allow the unfettered exportation of profits to absentee landlords. Such decapitalization of the local economy obviously boosts the power of the absentee landlords. However, some local development schemes, sponsored for example by the Overseas Development Administration, although in no way challenging the predominant economic patterns, do support the 'nationalistic' call for diversification. Perhaps the failure of these schemes illustrates the relative power of international interests over the local interest groups.

It could be argued that it is the 'nationalist' lobby, supported in Britain by the Falkland Island Committee, which has been the most important force in consistently opposing negotiations with Argentina. They have found widespread support from the 'unholy alliance' of left and right MPs in the British parliament. Their opposition to Argentina is based on a concern for what a change in sovereignty would mean to the social and cultural norms of the islands. For the absentee landlords however, the position seems less clear. Although they have all opposed negotiations, it is possible to argue that an Argentine take-over would not effect their vital interests. As long as Argentina did not seek to expropriate the foreign assets or to alter radically the economic *status quo* then the absentee landlords' basic interests would be safeguarded. Given the penetration of foreign capital in the Argentine economy and similar agricultural patterns this would seem unlikely. Furthermore, if oil, the major development possibility, is to be exploited, events have already shown that this can only take place after some kind of political agreement with Argentina has been reached. It would clearly be in the interests of the Falkland Island Company and its parent, Coalite, for the oil industry to be developed, since the islands are in a unique position in the South Atlantic to act as a base and supply point for the industry.

The Falkland Island Company

Since its formation in 1851, the Falkland Island Company (FIC) has been the main actor determining the shape of economic development in the islands. A brief examination of its history gives an insight into how the internationalization of capital has contributed to the creation of what we term an 'underdeveloped' area.

A Royal Charter of 22 December 1851, granted to 'Samuel Fisher Lafone, of Monte Video in South America' the right to buy land on East Falkland and granted him the 'absolute right to and exclusive dominion over all wild horses, horned cattle, sheep, goats and swine upon the Falkland Islands'. Lafone paid a total of £30,000 for this concession and agreed to provide the islands' governor with as many cattle as he required, free of charge, until 1856. Lafone enlisted the support of William Boutcher and John Hackblock in selling the 1,000 shares at £100 each needed to raise the capital for his venture. One interesting note on the Charter forbade the FIC to invest more than £2,000 in Britain.

The company's early years were anything but successful. Bad local management and the unwillingness of the Board of Directors in London to allow new lines of business (for example, the supplying of passing ships, or the salvaging of wrecks) hindered its development. The local manager complained bitterly of the business he was losing to J.M. Dean of Pebble Island, who had both the ready cash and the authority to make lucrative deals with passing ships. For a time it looked as though the FIC would falter, leaving the local economy to the four other farmers who were working the land in 1862. It is interesting to note that of the four, Captain Packe, Mr Pitaluga and Mr Dean have left their names on three family farms that still operate on the islands.

However, the FIC was soon able to take a dominant position in the Falklands' economy by raising capital in Britain. In 1902 it became a limited company and increased its capital by 50 per cent. This capital was used to purchase land on the islands. For example, in 1920, the FIC paid £155,000 in its own shares to Vere Packe for 68,000 acres of land. Vere Packe became a director of the company. The company further extended its influence by establishing linking directorships with other farming companies. So, for example, in 1948 the company had linking directorships with eight other companies, two of which, Holmestead Blake and Co. Ltd and J.L. Waldron Ltd, today share the FIC's London office.

The company found, however, that relying totally on Falklands wool production for its profits was not good business. In order to broaden the company's income base and thus provide a cushion against low farm profits at times of depressed wool prices, the company started to invest in Britain, in ships chandling, warehousing and automatic vending machines.

This diversification stage in the company's history could be said to have started in February 1962, when the FIC became a public limited company whose shares were freely traded on the London Stock Exchange. Although the FIC's shareholders had predominantly been non-islanders, the company's success was intimately bound up with the success of the Falklands wool industry. In addition, the number of local shareholders and directors ensured that the FIC policy was aligned to local development objectives as defined by local landowners. However, from 1962 onwards, shares were increasingly held by non-islanders. By 1968 it was reported that there were 800 shareholders in the UK and only 70 to 80 in the Falklands. The influence of the Falkland shareholders was therefore, slowly declining. The non-islander directors were quite happy that profit from the Falklands be reinvested elsewhere, thus hastening the process of decapitalization of the islands, which has become the dominant feature of the economy.

The declining profitability of the wool industry also discouraged investment in the islands and the FIC accumulated a substantial cash balance and portfolio investments (that is, holdings of shares of other companies) which were not reflected in its share value. It was therefore ripe for takeover, and in 1972 a subsidiary of Slater Walker Securities, the Dundee, Perth and London Shipping Company, bought the FIC from its previous shareholders for £3.5 million. Although the reason for the takeover was stated as being an interest in a FIC subsidiary, Southern Ships Stores Ltd, there could have been other motives. The early 1970s was the heyday of the 'asset strippers'. They would buy a company, sell off its profitable parts and then resell what remained of the company. The theory was that the company was worth more when split into its component parts than as a whole. So, between 1972 when it was purchased and 1973 when it was resold, £500,000 in cash, and portfolio investments with a market value of £489,607, were transferred from the FIC to its parent company.

The irony of the situation was that at the same time as 'decapitalization' of the islands was taking on an altogether different meaning at the hands of Slater Walker, the government's pension fund held over £6,000 worth of Slater Walker shares.

The FIC shareholders were thus no longer people who had a historical or emotional link to the Falklands. The investment in the islands was now to be judged solely on its income yielding potential for its shareholders. Faced with a declining wool industry, the shareholders chose to withdraw their profits from the islands and invest them in more lucrative opportunities elsewhere. When Mr Michael Buckley, a member of the board of Dundee, London and Perth Ltd, asked if any of the £700,000 profit generated by the FIC might be ploughed back, he was told that there was little to spend the money on. 'Maybe £30,000 on fencing, that's all'. This was at the same time as Dundee, London and Perth were withdrawing the islands' only shipping link with the outside world, much to the distress of the islanders.

In 1973, the FIC changed hands for a second time and became part of Charringtons Industrial Holdings. In 1974, the FIC accounts listed seven companies as being wholly or partly owned. These companies had been bought during the FIC's diversification phase and had to a large extent been paid for with profits generated in the Falklands. By the time of the 1976 accounts, four of these companies, Southern Ships Stores Ltd, J.G. Boyes (Vending) Ltd, J.G. Boyes (Warehousing) Ltd, and H.G. Goodwin Ltd had all been transferred to the parent company. In 1977, Charringtons was acquired by the Coalite Group (which, among other things, produced dioxin, used in the manufacture of the banned herbicide 2,4,5-T and the defoliant Agent Orange which was extensively used in Vietnam) and the FIC became an even less significant part of a still larger company. In 1981, the FIC sales of £3 million represented no more than 2 per cent of Coalite's total business. And Coalite's latest annual report illustrates how the Falklands' wool industry continues to be run down: 'With increasing production costs and depressed wool prices, the returns from sheep farming in the Falkland Islands have deteriorated'.

The net result of all the changes that have befallen the FIC mean that no islanders are now represented either as shareholders or directors of the company currently controlling the FIC. And although the FIC retains a monopolistic grip on the islands, the objectives of the Coalite board are clearly at odds with those who aim for any form of integral development for the islands. From the islanders' point of view, not only have they lost their say in the way that FIC is run, but on 21 April 1982, they even lost the right to examine its accounts or know who owns it. At an Extraordinary Meeting on 26 February 1982 it was decided that the FIC would no longer be registered as a public limited company. It is therefore no longer obliged to publish the sort of information that the islanders might need if they are to influence it in any way.

The Company Monopoly

Although the islanders have lost control of the FIC, the reverse unfortunately is not the case. The FIC retains its monopolistic control over the islands. By directly owning 42 per cent of the islands' land

and by linking directorships with other independent farming companies, the FIC accounts for 66 per cent of the sheep sheared on the islands. It is also able to influence other independent companies by way of the positions it holds in the Sheep Owners' Association. As well as marketing its own wool clip, the FIC also markets a substantial proportion of the independent wool producers clip, by way of a wholly owned subsidiary. It operates the only sea link with the UK, an essential element in getting the wool to market. The company dominates wholesale and retail distribution on the islands. West Stores, the company supermarket in Port Stanley, accounts for over 50 per cent of all the retail trade on the islands. The two inshore freighters, which given the non-existent road network are essential for freight traffic, are owned or managed by the FIC. Nor can their influence on the local government be underestimated, given that they contribute a large proportion of government revenue in the form of company tax. The FIC's monopoly control of the islands encouraged Lord Shackleton to comment:

Furthermore, it should be carefully considered, in the light of the dominant role played by the FIC in the economy, whether the Falklands government ought not to be in a position to influence, if not control, the company's policy . . . (so) that the public interest is safeguarded.

Decapitalization

If there is one cause of the decline in population and in the Falkland Island economy, it is the drain of resources from the Falklands to the UK. Given the choice between local reinvestment of after-tax profits and investment in the UK, the companies have chosen the latter option.
Shackleton Report.

The profits being generated by the islanders on the sheep ranches are not being retained and reinvested in the local economy. Rather, the absentee landowners (and especially Coalite) are withdrawing their profits and investing them in other activities in Britain and elsewhere. This means that funds are not available locally to create new jobs that would halt the depopulation of the islands. Nor is there capital for local infrastructure, roads, improved education facilities and entertainment that would improve the quality of life for the islanders.

The Shackleton Report looks in some detail at this decapitalization, the root of the Falklands decline. Examining the private farming companies, he estimated that between 1970 and 1973, they distributed 59 per cent of their after-tax profits to their shareholders. Of the profits retained in the companies, rather than being used for new machinery or improvements to the farms, 86 per cent was used to purchase shares on the British and US stock exchanges. With so little

17

investment in the farms, there was insufficient capital available to replace existing machinery, let alone to invest in projects that could lead to economic diversification.

A brief look at the 1980 accounts of one of the locally-owned farming companies will illustrate how little investment is being directed back into the wool industry. Packe Bros and Co. reported total assets in 1980 of £346,000. Of this, no less than £147,560 was in the form of investments outside the islands. These investments yielded a profit of £12,800, whereas the sheep farm recorded a loss of £6,361. The directors were recommending that the farm be sold.

The FIC illustrates a similar pattern. In 1977, out of post-tax profits of £290,000, dividends paid amounted to £208,000 and in 1978, of £270,385 post-tax profit, £218,000 was distributed as a dividend to overseas shareholders . . . namely Coalite.

This decapitalization would not be so serious for the islands if it were being balanced out by capital flowing back in the form, for example, of UK assistance. However, over the period 1951 to 1974, the export of company profits was more than three-and-a-half times greater than the inflow of UK government assistance. In fact, it is estimated that companies operating in the Falklands pay more in British taxes than the UK government distributes in aid to the islands. The UK aid has increased over the past few years, especially to cover the cost of the permanent airstrip (which has subsequently been denounced as a white elephant as it is too small for all but local traffic), and a school hostel (see Table 3, page 128). The latter has been the subject of continuing controversy. Contracted to a FIC subsidiary, the plan was to use a system of construction involving concrete sprayed onto metal latticework. This has not been successful and apart from costing three times the original estimate, the hostel has still not been declared fit for human habitation. Projects of this type are hardly likely to have a decisive effect on the state of the local economy.

This situation led Lord Shackleton to conclude in his 1976 report:

Fiscal policy should be designed so as to encourage the retention and reinvestment of company profits (in the islands) . . . there can be little justification for any future UK aid related to the private sector, if its sole net effect is to increase the remittance of profits to the UK.

Development plans

In the face of this slow but steady decline in the islands' economy, various proposals have been put forward to reverse the trend. However, due to both external political problems and the nature of the internal economy, little progress has been made.

It has been suggested that the Falkland Islands lie in what could shortly become a major oil-producing region. Air Commodore Frowe, of the Falkland Island Committee, has argued that this was the main motivation for the Argentine invasion. The oil potential of the area involves two distinct regions, firstly that in and around the islands themselves and especially in the waters between the Falklands and the mainland; secondly, the potential of Antarctica to the south.

Oil finds near the coast of Argentina by Shell, Exxon and Total have so far been disappointing. *Petroleum Information*, an oil industry publication, stated in April 1982 that oil exploration near the Falklands had not disclosed any major reserves. However, it said that exploration work was continuing and the companies were showing interest in moving their rigs further to the east and therefore closer to the islands. A Canadian survey team indicated that there could be several prospective oil-bearing areas around the Falklands, but British attempts to sell exploration concessions in these areas have been contested by Argentina. Similar Argentine attempts to sell concessions in disputed areas were challenged by Britain. It is clear that any further exploration will not take place until a political solution to the current crisis has been found. During the crisis the last of the three foreign drilling rigs operating in the area, Shell's Interocean-2, was towed to safety out of the war zone.

The oil and mineral wealth in Antarctica represents an altogether different picture. The oil potential of the area, according to a US Geological Survey, could be anything between 15 and 50 billion barrels, though the technology needed to recover these reserves will not be available for some years. Britain's territorial interests in Antarctica, in the so-called British Antarctic Territories, conflict with territorial claims made by both Chile and Argentina. The basis of the respective claims are quite different. Chile and Argentina project lines from the east and west extremities of their territories south to the pole. The British claim (as with the Australian, New Zealand, French and Norwegian claims) is based on the right to occupy and claim any unoccupied land, which has been used in the past as the legal justification for much European territorial expansion. There is little doubt however, that sovereign control of the Falklands and its dependent territories strengthens the British claim. Also, from a practical point of view, Port Stanley is an important supply point for the British Antarctic Survey team working in the area, and for any future schemes to develop the continent's undoubted resources.

Interest has been shown in various projects aimed at harvesting and processing the giant seaweed (kelp) that abounds around the islands. Processing the kelp produces alginates which are extensively used in the food, textile and paper industries. So far no progress has been made in developing these resources and it would appear that discussions about them were limited to those occasions when Britain and Argentina were making headway in their negotiations over the future of the islands. In 1968, for instance, Alginate Industries Ltd confirmed that the kelp could generate a viable local industry with annual sales of £12 million. However, they added that there would be no progress if Britain ceded sovereignty to Argentina. The British government considered the scheme as no more than a remote possibility. Again, in 1977, Alginate Industries was talking of a plant with a capacity of 5,000 tons employing 35 people. The islands' Legislative Council was told in February 1977 that the company held out glowing prospects for the scheme. However, by June the company was surrendering its licences due to the British government's 'ill-timed approaches to the Argentine government'.

Plans to develop a fishing industry around the Falklands have also been suggested, but so far they have failed to produce any results. The *Shackleton Report* estimated that there are no less than 80 varieties of fish around the islands and that commercially significant shoals of hake, croaker, blue whiting and Falkland herring were available. It suggested that a feasibility study be carried out to test fish the waters in the area. Polish, Russian and Japanese boats at present operate in the area. A potentially far more important marine resource is the immense quantities of krill, a crustacean similar to a shrimp, that are to be found around South Georgia and to the south. According to the British Antarctic Survey, present day reserves of krill in the region far exceed the existing world fish catch. As yet, only 200,000 tons a year are being caught. Krill was the food that sustained the large whale population in the area in the 1960s and 1970s and it is estimated that today whales, seals and sea birds consume 100 million tons per year. It is a rich source of protein that could become an important part of the human diet in the near future.

Plans to diversify the islands' agriculture have been drawn up, but again no concrete results have been obtained. Back in the 1920s the Anson Experimental Farm at Green Patch looked likely to give a lead. However, it was closed down in 1928 and the Falklands government has had no effective Agriculture Department since the 1950s. The British government is sponsoring a Grasslands Trials Unit in an attempt to improve the quality of the pasture. Other improvements that have been suggested include changes in pasture utilization, increased mechanization, an examination of sheep breeding and selection methods and agricultural diversification. So far none of these have been implemented.

In the conclusion to his economic and social report on the Falkland Islands in 1976, Lord Shackleton underlined that there would be no possibility of any real development until the islands' airport was strengthened and extended so that it could handle international traffic. He emphasized that all the other development possibilities he had made hinged upon this factor. His recommendation was not accepted. Ironically enough however, the airport has now been extended to accommodate British military aircraft.

However, the *Shackleton Report* fails to emphasize the two fundamental reforms that are needed before any economic development will occur. The first concerns ownership of the land. As long as the islands' agricultural land remains in the hands of absentee landlords who use it for a form of agriculture that has little long-term viability, then there can be no development on the islands. For such landowners, who measure their success in terms of the dividend they receive, there is no incentive either to invest more in sheep farming or to invest in agricultural diversification. And it is only in such diversification that the islands' economy can hope to have a future. As one local farm owner commented: 'You can go on ranching indefinitely, but it's stagnation. The profit margins get less and less'.

The need for some kind of land reform has been accepted by the Falkland Islands government. So far this has taken the form of attempts to split up large ranches into smaller holdings that would be available for local families. This would both stop the continual loss of population and encourage diversification by more intense farming. The first farm to be split was Green Patch, bought by the Falklands government for £170,000 from the FIC. And the local government had clear ideas of what it was hoping to achieve: 'If the people who take over the farm — or the units — have ideas of ranching as it has always been done in the colony, this will be of no benefit, it will not be development'. A second farm, Roy Cove, also bought by the government, is to be sold in six sections at £60,000 to £80,000 per section.

This, of course, is merely the tip of the iceberg. Offering sections of land for sale for tens of thousands of pounds is hardly likely to benefit the average farm labourer. If the islands are to remain inhabited into the future, with a population above the critical minimum needed to ensure its viability, then the massive land holdings of the foreign-owned companies must be appropriated and redistributed among those who at present work them.

The second critical reform that is needed concerns the government of the islands. Such a small community cannot afford the dubious luxury of a colonial bureaucracy. The present system of government, the Executive and Legislative Councils, was described by *The Times* of 22 March 1976, as a 'virtually undemocratic body, which is slow and inefficient'. What little democratic participation it does entail merely allows the local landowners and farm managers a small voice in the islands' government. Lack of education, quasi-feudal social relations and the predominant paternalism that exists, keep the majority of the islanders out of the political life of the community.

Within the logic of the prevailing economic conditions the islands now face even less chance of economic development than before the war. Peaceful coexistence and cooperation with Argentina, the constantly repeated pre-requisite for development, now looks a remote possibility. However, even if the political problems could be resolved, the Shackleton proposals do not confront the underlying problems. His attempts to attract both British government funds and private investment to the islands failed and will fail again precisely because the islands are not competitive from a purely capitalist point of view due to the years of decapitalization and underinvestment that they have suffered, nor are they of any long-term political or strategic importance to Britain. Land reform and investment that aims to create local jobs rather than merely generate profits for absentee landlords can be the only basis on which the islands have an economic future.

These limitations to the development of the islands economy apply equally whether sovereignty is transferred to Argentina or remains British. There is no reason to believe that Argentina would apply a different development model than the one at present in operation.

2 A Question of Power: Claim and Counterclaim

'There is a certain futility in interposing the lean and ascetic visage of the law in a situation which, first and last, is merely a question of power.'
Julius Goebel, *The Struggle for the Falkland Islands* (Yale, 1927).*

In 1767 Father Sebastian Villanueva described the new Spanish colony on the Falkland Islands as an 'unhappy desert'. More recently, former US Secretary of State Alexander Haig described the islands as a 'pimple on the ass of progress'. Yet these apparently insignificant and uninviting islands have been at the centre of a major international conflagration in which over a thousand people have lost their lives.

The debate about sovereignty over the Falkland Islands has raged throughout the war in the South Atlantic. Many of the issues have been obscured by the polemical and emotional nature of the argument. The British Foreign and Commonwealth Office, for instance, produced a pamphlet for popular consumption entitled *The Falkland Islands: The Facts*, which aimed at presenting the British case. On the issue of sovereignty, it blandly states: 'British governments have never doubted the validity of the British claim to sovereignty over the Falkland Islands and Dependencies. In 1690 the British Captain Strong made the first recorded landing on the Falkland Islands . . .'

In reality a number of British governments have had doubts about the British case, which is highly contentious in terms of international law. In 1910, a member of the Foreign Office research department, Gaston de Bernhardt, produced a 17,000-word memo at the behest of

*Julius Goebel, *The Struggle for the Falkland Islands* was reprinted by Yale University Press in 1982 with a preface and introduction by J.C.J. Metford. It provides the most thoroughly researched account of the countervailing claims of the different powers until 1833.

the head of the Foreign Office's American department, Sidney Spicer. The memo, which became the standard Foreign Office paper on the issue for the next two decades, seriously questioned the view that the British had a clear-cut claim to the islands. In the words of Spicer: 'From a perusal of this memo, it is difficult to avoid the conclusion that the Argentine government's attitude is not altogether unjustified and that our action has been somewhat high-handed'.

The existence of such doubts was discovered by Peter Beck, a senior lecturer in politics at the Kingston Polytechnic, who wrote an article on the subject in the *Journal of Inter-American Studies and World Affairs* in February 1982. Since the hostilities, however, many of the records which Beck consulted at the Public Record Office in London have been closed to public scrutiny by the Foreign Office.

Neither the British nor the Argentine governments have wanted to take the issue of sovereignty to the International Court of Justice at The Hague because there is no certainty as to which way the decision would go. The relationship of the sovereignty issue to present-day international law is undoubtedly complex. But perhaps there is a more important aspect to the Falkland Islands question than its legal implications, namely the historical context in which Britain asserted its claim in the first place.

This context involves the power relations between Britain and Spain in the first instance, and subsequently between Britain and Argentina. The legal arguments must be examined against this background, since only then is it possible to understand the basis for the strong feeling in Argentina and the rest of Latin America about the validity of the Argentine claim.

Discovery and settlement

The discovery of the islands is itself a point of contention between the two countries, exacerbated by the sketchy nature of the data on the early voyages to the South Atlantic. The first navigator to go to this region was Amerigo Vespucci, and he is given the credit for the discovery of the islands in 1504. The British have claimed that two English navigators, John Davis and Richard Hawkins, in separate voyages, discovered the islands in the sixteenth century.

The scholar who has investigated the issue most thoroughly, Julius Goebel, concludes the following:

With one exception there has been a lamentable failure to treat these two accounts (of Davis' and Hawkins' expeditions) with any degree of scientific scepticism. This is probably due to the fact that the British writers who have concerned themselves most with their two compatriots have instinctively awarded them a greater deference than they would feel toward alien navigators. Nevertheless, in view of the slight and rather inaccurate data given by Davis and Hawkins, there is very little reason for being dogmatic in the claim that one of the two discovered the Falklands.

The islands were in fact not fixed on the charts until the voyage of the Dutchman Sebald de Weert to the area in 1600.

The historical background to the early voyages, up to the settlement of the islands in the mid-eighteenth century, has considerable relevance to the subsequent debate over sovereignty. The essential characteristic of this period was the struggle between Spain and Britain for control of the Americas. Spanish maritime superiority had enabled Spain to conquer the New World in the sixteenth century. Spain had sought to secure its rights to the area first of all against its major rival, Portugal. The Papal Bull of 1493 and the Treaty of Tordesillas the following year delimited the Spanish and Portuguese colonizations. Spanish rights in the New World thus rested initially on papal decrees, and subsequently, as the rise of protestantism undermined the value of these, on occupation and conquest.

The only way other nations could benefit from the colonizations of the New World after the Spanish conquest was through trade, which the Spanish sought to control. Once the French and English were able to challenge Spanish naval superiority, it became very difficult for Spain to assert its closed sea policy, which had previously enabled it to control foreign maritime activities by force.

During the reign of Elizabeth I of England (1558-1603), French corsairs and English freebooters such as Francis Drake were challenging the Spanish trade monopoly. Following the defeat of the Spanish Armada in 1588, the struggle between a declining Spain and an emergent England intensified. Spain now sought recognition of its right to its colonies and maritime access to them was arranged by treaty. Over the next century and a half, the frequent wars between the European powers were interspersed with attempts by the rival states to regulate their relations, including domestic colonial policies, by means of treaty law.

Whereas during the recent crisis the British have preferred to emphasize the continuous occupation of the islands since 1833, the Argentinians have looked back to those years of the Spanish empire when the series of international treaties which established the 'public law' of Europe also secured international recognition and acceptance of Spain's colonial possessions and the surrounding waters.

Closed Seas and Pirates

The most thorough investigation of the implications of these treaties and their relevance to the struggle for the islands is again to be found in Goebel's study. He examines the effects of each treaty since the Peace of Westphalia of 1648, which established the principle of *uti possidetis*. This gave the colonial powers (principally Spain and the Netherlands) the right of sovereignty over all territory then in their actual possession. This weakened Spanish claims to unoccupied lands in the Americas in cases where other powers could claim a legal title by virtue of previous conquest or peaceful settlement.

Spain therefore acted to prevent such claims being made by restricting access to the shores and high seas around its territories. Although the limits of the 'closed sea' were never determined, during the next century Spain dedicated much of its energies to enforcing the idea and having the principle accepted in international treaties. By conceding to her enemies the actual conquests made by them during various European wars, Spain succeeded in asserting the 'closed sea' principle in every treaty from 1667 to the French revolution. It therefore became illegal to acquire colonies in the Spanish sphere of influence during peacetime.

The English government never officially broke the treaties, but it was English pirates who tried to resist the implications of the treaties and maintained the English challenge to the Spanish empire. Goebel points out how the success of one of the English buccaneers, Captain Morgan, in capturing Panama encouraged other exploits, this time further south:

the ease with which this great centre of Spanish trade on the Pacific had fallen and the vastness of the booty suggested to the fertile imaginations of these empire-builders the glowing prospect of unlimited and lucrative business in the South Seas. It was in persuance of this dream, already carried out by others, that an expedition was organized which again brought the English into the environs of the Falklands.

A number of buccaneers from Virginia, led by Captain John Cook and William Damper, set off for the South Atlantic, discovering what was probably one of the Falkland Islands in 1684. They reported the existence of a large harbour, exciting the British Admiralty with visions of a naval establishment in the region, from where it could extend British commercial influence on Spanish possessions. But the treaties of 1667 and 1670 made such an undertaking illegal.

However in 1690, at a time when England and Spain were allies in a war against France, some of the rules on the sheltering of privateers were waived by the Spanish, and the English took advantage of this to make further inroads into the Spanish trade monopoly. The admiralty issued a privateers commission for an expedition against the French, and using this document, several English merchants joined together to equip a ship to raid Spanish settlements and search for treasure from ships wrecked off the Pacific coast. Amongst them was Captain John Strong, who in 1690 was the first Englishman to land on the islands, and gave them their present name in English (see page 00). But Strong's landing had no legal implication and did not involve any formal occupation of the islands as it was a clear violation of existing treaties.

It should be mentioned here too that England was not the only country attempting to break the Spanish trade monopoly. During the wars between France and Spain, the French sailors and traders operating out of St Malo, mostly with official recognition, engaged in a lucrative contraband trade in the South Atlantic throughout the late seventeenth century. A number of French navigators visited the area in the early 1700s, but the ending of the War of Spanish Succession in Europe meant an end to these explorations.

The Treaty of Utrecht in 1713 again reaffirmed the principle of *uti possidetis*, and access to the seas around Spanish possessions in South and Central America was still refused in the treaties. According to Goebel, 'it was the frustration of the English dream of a great overseas commerce carried on under the rose that led to the adoption of a policy of territorial aggrandizement which included the first seizure of the Falkland Islands'.

The second half of the eighteenth century saw increased tension between England and Spain. In 1759 Charles III ascended the throne of Spain and ordered an enquiry into the economy of the Spanish empire. The report presented to him in 1761 concluded that 'by far the worst offenders of all in the contraband trade (which is the root of so many disorders in Your Majesty's dominions) are the English'. Charles III determined to reduce the opportunities for foreigners to benefit automatically from Spain's overseas colonies and to increase the opportunities for Spanish traders, many of whom had been unable to participate in the commerce because of the exclusive monopoly over the trade by the narrow commercial interests of Seville and Cadiz.

These tensions between Britain and Spain led to war between the two countries when Spain joined France against Britain in the Seven Years' War. The war ended in 1763 with the Treaty of Paris. Spain lost Minorca and Florida, and French power in North America was eliminated.

Britain had already begun to consider ways in which it could extend its commercial penetration of Spain's colonies more directly. One method it employed was to establish free ports and offshore bases around the Spanish empire. The Falkland Islands were considered a very good base for interrupting Spanish trade.

In the late 1740s the British government planned to send two frigates on a mission to explore the Falkland Islands. When the Spanish government complained that Britain had no possessions in the South Seas and therefore had no right to send the frigates there, the British justified the expedition by claiming that it was regarded as a purely scientific project.

The Duke of Bedford wrote in 1749:

As there is no intention of making any settlement in either of those islands, and as His Majesty's sloops will neither touch upon or even make any part of the Spanish coast, the king can in no shape apprehend that this Design can give any umbrage at Madrid.

This idea seems to have come out of the experience of Admiral Anson, who in 1740 during the war with Spain, had attempted to sail round the Horn to capture ports on the Pacific coast. But the lack of a convenient naval base made such a campaign impossible. The difficulties of rounding the Horn led Anson to reflect on the usefulness of a base south of Brazil both to facilitate the passage and for future operations aimed at interrupting the Spanish trade. He suggested that an expedition be sent to survey the Falkland Islands:

If on examination, . . . these places should appear proper for the purpose intended, it is scarcely to be conceived of what prodigious import a convenient station might prove situated so far to the southward and so near to Cape Horn.

The statement illustrates the degree to which the British had accepted that various treaties gave them no right to send the frigates, and the expedition was abandoned.

Eighteenth century colonization

The next stage in the saga involved the French. Louis XV's foreign minister, the Duc de Choiseul, was anxious to restore the French overseas empire. He accepted a proposal by Antoine-Louis de Bougainville to mount an expedition to the Falklands with the help of St Malo sailors, who already knew the islands well. The objective would be to establish a staging post for French penetration of the Pacific.

The expedition arrived in 1764 and formal possession of the islands was taken in the name of Louis XV. A small colony was established on East Falkland at Port Louis. Spain was immediately alerted.

At the time the Spanish were considering a proposal to fortify the islands in order to protect Spanish trade since they commanded the Magellan Straits and Cape Horn. They informed Choiseul that a

French settlement at Port Louis would harm Spanish interests by encouraging the British to attempt a similar scheme. The Spanish based their legal argument on territorial proximity. Eventually the French, allies of Spain, agreed to transfer the islands to Spain in exchange for a large sum of money in compensation. In 1767 the islands were formally ceded to Spain and a Spanish governor appointed.

Meanwhile the British too had decided to send an expedition to the islands with the same purpose as before, to use them as a base for disrupting Spanish trade. Commodore John Byron, grandfather of the poet, arrived in West Falkland in January 1765 and took possession of the islands in the name of King George II. He established a settlement at Port Egmont, so-called after the Earl of Egmont, the First Lord of the Admiralty. Byron knew nothing of the French settlement and in his survey of the island did not discover it. He wrote to England that there were no signs of any other people on the islands. On receiving the news, the British government planned an immediate settlement.

On 20 July 1765 Lord Egmont wrote to the Duke of Grafton, then Secretary of State for the Northern Department, stating that proof of the British title to the islands was complete. In fact, at this stage the British based their claim on discovery, although no legal grounds supporting this in the laws between nations existed at that time. Egmont wrote:

The perusal of the enclosures . . . will also show the great importance of this station, which is undoubtedly the key to the whole Pacific Ocean. This Island must command the Ports and trade of Chile, Peru, Panama, Acapulco and in one word all the Spanish Territory upon that sea. It will render all our expeditions to those parts most lucrative to ourselves, most fatal to Spain and no longer formidable, tedious or uncertain in a future war . . . Your Grace will presently perceive the prodigious use hereafter to be made of an establishment in this place by that nation who shall first fix a firm footing there.

This letter illustrates the importance of taking into account the historical background to the Falkland Islands issue. Far from asserting an irrefutable right of sovereignty over the islands, what motivated the British was their search for markets and, in particular, their desire to break the Spanish trade monopoly in Central and South America.

A British expedition was sent to reinforce Byron's settlement under the command of John McBride, arriving in the Falklands in January 1766, two years after the French had landed and fourteen months before the Spanish took possession.

It was McBride who discovered the French settlement some months later. He delivered a warning to the French to leave and then himself returned to England. The British government had been informed in May 1776 that the French colony had been transferred to Spain. Goebel claims, on the basis of dispatches from the French *chargé d'affaires* Durand — who gained his information from bribing a clerk in the admiralty — that in fact the British knew all along that a French colony had been established on the Falklands and that France claimed sovereignty. In his view, this is why the British were forced to assert their claim by virtue of discovery rather than occupation, despite its lack of legal validity. When the British dispatched a fleet to secure Port Egmont, it was clear that they were ready to go to war rather than give up the colony.

According to Goebel the Spanish at this time seem to have asserted their rights to the islands on the basis of the Treaty of Utrecht, which had confirmed the premise that possession was the only true index of title which itself had been expressed most fully in the American Treaty of 1670. Article 8 of the Treaty of Utrecht withheld permission for France or any other nation to sail to any of the dominions of Spain in the Americas and it aimed to leave navigation and commerce in the same state as it had been in the time of Charles II of Spain. Spain regarded any approach to her territories in the South Atlantic or the Pacific as a violation of the treaty. Spanish protests, when they occurred, such as in 1749 over the proposed British mission to the islands, were usually successful. Goebel concludes that: 'Under such an interpretation of the treaty, therefore, the conclusion is inescapable that an expedition to the Falklands was in direct violation of the terms of the Treaty of Utrecht and of the express guarantee pledged by England in 1713'.

He then considers whether the islands could be considered Spanish territory. He does not see geographical propinquity as a strong argument since the islands are a long way from the South American coast. He argues however that as the Treaty of Utrecht prohibited navigation in the southern waters there is some justification in regarding the Falklands as included in the *status quo* agreement of the Treaty, 'for if access to the place was denied, *a fortiori*, a colony was not to be considered'.

The other aspect of legal claims to the islands is that of prior occupation. There is no doubt that the French settled the islands two years before the English reached Port Egmont and were the first occupiers. But the Spanish challenged the French right to be there and could well claim their own assertion of sovereignty as original title and not derived from the French cession of the islands. Spain did not claim its own occupation of 1767 as the basis of title as this was subsequent to the British occupation. If the British did not recognize the Treaty of Utrecht as applicable, they were bound to regard the French occupation as prior and accept the cession of the Falklands to Spain which gave them derivative sovereignty. This Goebel regards as the strongest claim from the legal point of view as it is free from the political ambiguities of the Treaty of Utrecht. Thus Goebel concludes:

Leaving aside the contentious point of the application of the Treaty of Utrecht, the British right rested merely on discovery, a wholly unsupportable ground, for the Spanish, having succeeded to any title of the French, were in law to be treated as prior occupants. On the other hand, if we admit the treaty applied, the whole British position is demolished . . .

From what has been said, there can be no doubt but that at the beginning of the year 1770 the British were on the Falklands without the least color of right and that their act in making settlement was one of pure aggression, involving not merely a denial of the validity of a previous settlement by another power, but likewise the repudiation of a solemn treaty engagement which had subsisted for over a half-century.

Supporters of the British claim to the islands tend not to dwell on these arguments but concentrate on the events which followed the British determination to secure their colony. In 1770 the governor of Buenos Aires ordered an attack on the British settlement at Port Egmont, but the French who were still Spain's close allies were unprepared to go to war over the island. Eventually an agreement was reached between the Spanish and the British under which the former restored West Falkland to the British. Controversy surrounds this agreement. In 1834 Lord Palmerston in a letter to Manuel Moreno, the Argentine ambassador to Britain, justifying Britain's seizure of the islands, claimed that in 1771 Spain recognized British sovereignty over the islands. The Argentinians contended that the Spanish withdrew both to avoid war and because they had received a secret promise from Lord North, the British prime minister at the time, that if Spain withdrew and satisfied British honour and Lord North's own political position, after a time Britain would leave. Palmerston stated that there was no evidence to support this assertion. Goebel places much emphasis on the existence of the secret promise, although Metford in his preface to the new edition of Goebel's work cites his failure to prove the existence of such an agreement as one of its weaknesses. Most of the evidence comes from Spanish and French dispatches which 'proves no more' in the words of Metford, than that the Spanish negotiator was under the impression that the British would withdraw once they had received satisfaction. However, De Bernhardt in his 1910 memo makes specific reference to this issue and notes that Palmerston had examined only the 'official correspondence' when seeking evidence of a promise to Spain. Goebel also makes the point that Lord Shelbourne, Secretary of State at the time of the agreement, had a policy of ensuring that no embarrassing papers were kept in the archives. De Bernhardt clearly gave credence to the idea that such an agreement had existed and also made the point that the key question of sovereignty was specifically excluded from the 1771 agreement with Spain.

In any case, the British did withdraw from Port Egmont in 1774, leaving a plaque and the British flag to assert their rights. Metford claims the withdrawal was for reasons of economy. Goebel points out that the existence of the plaque had no legal relevance at all and had 'no more bearing on the fact of possession than if it had never been left there'. He maintains that as Britain had no right to the islands under the rules of occupation or existing European treaties 'the existence of the treaties and the fact that they were not expressly repudiated is important proof of the view that the abandonment of Port Egmont was an abandonment in law as well as in fact:

. . . this . . . seems to the writer to strip the British claim to the island after abandonment of all legal quality. Any merit that their claim may have had depended upon their ability to show prior occupation as well as a right to enter (the area) under the Treaty of Utrecht, and as the restoration of their colony was expressly stated to be no more than an act of satisfaction for an injury to the British crown, this restoration did not supply legal validity to a claim which had from the first lacked foundation . . . the abandonment of Port Egmont really disposed of any shadow of right which the British may have had.

In 1790, furthermore, the Nootka Sound Convention between England and Spain pledged both parties not to establish new colonies in the South Atlantic. What was already occupied was to remain in the occupant's possession provided no third party attempted to settle in regions not already occupied, thus reiterating the principle of *uti posseditis*. Goebel states that this had a significant bearing upon the legal status of the Falklands at that time; 'The British had now in a solemn treaty recognized the *status quo*; the *de facto* occupation of the whole Falkland group was admitted by them to be an occupation in the legal sense'.

Following the British withdrawal from West Falkland the Spanish appointed a succession of governors and took measures to preserve its sovereignty. The British showed no interest in the islands during the next 55 years.

Independence, Invasion, and Commerce

Britain did however retain its interest in South America. It was evident by the time of the Falkland Island dispute that the possibilities for further encroachment on the Spanish American trade by illegal means were reaching their limits. In addition the market for British goods in the region had reached the point where it could expand no further, due to the poverty of the colonies and local self-sufficiency.

The British had not abandoned the use of force and colonization to back up commercial ends despite the loss of its North American colonies in 1783. But there were few who advocated the acquisition of direct empire in Spanish America, since the costs was considered to be much in excess of the benefits. So in the 1790s Britain continued its illegal trade, particularly in the Rio de la Plata region. The Spanish had created a viceroyalty of the Rio de la Plata in 1776 and a tempting new market.

It was not until 1790 when the Nootka Sound dispute nearly led to war between Spain and Britain that Britain considered attacking the Spanish colonies. It was at this time that the British Prime Minister, William Pitt, began to court some of the agitators for Spanish American liberation then living in London. However, when peace was signed by the two countries in October 1790 the agitators found themselves abandoned. 'I am sold', complained Miranda, subsequently to become one of the most important figures in the independence movement, 'by a treaty of commerce with Spain'.

In October 1796 Spain joined France in war against Britain and the British began again to consider an attack on the Spanish empire as well as assistance to the independence movement. Never far from government thinking were the commercial advantages in addition to the help in the war such action would bring. They were though, still very concerned by the social consequences of liberation in Spanish America and the influence of the French Revolution. Miranda reassured Pitt that the form of government of a liberated Spanish America would be 'very similar to that of Great Britain'. Plans for an expedition to Buenos Aires were initiated in 1801 but had still not been sanctioned by the cabinet when Pitt's administration fell that same year. The idea was not abandoned however. One man particularly concerned with how to pursue the disintegration of the Spanish Empire was Commodore Sir Home Popham of the Royal Navy. In 1804 he had been involved together with Viscount Melville in one of the many cabinet discussions on the subject. In a memorandum to Melville in October of that year, Popham spelt out the advantages:

The idea of conquering South America is totally out of the question, but the possibility of gaining all its prominent points, alienating it from its present European connections, fixing on some Military position and enjoying all its Commercial advantages can be reduced to a fair calculation, if not a certain operation; The Nerve and Spirit which such an Enterprise would give to this

Country if successful are incalculable. The riches that it would bring in, the new Sources that it would open for our Manufacturers and Navigation, both from Europe and Terra Firma, and from Asia to the Pacific, are equally incalculable, and the popularity and stability that it would give any Government that undertook it, may be estimated from the preceding propositions . . .

In 1806 Sir Home Popham led an unauthorized expedition which captured Buenos Aires. The Buenos Aires market alone would 'consume nearly two millions annually of our manufactures', declared Popham. The action was warmly greeted by the merchant houses of Britain. The town of Manchester passed a resolution: 'The capture of Buenos Aires has revived the drooping spirits of our merchants and manufacturers. The loom is again very busily employed'. The government succumbed to the enthusiasm and sent reinforcements. But the inhabitants of Buenos Aires did not want British rule and in 1807 expelled the occupying forces. The whole episode was important for two fundamental reasons. Firstly, it convinced the British that their best way to gain access to Latin American markets was to support the independence movements, not to colonize the area.

From now on British penetration of South America was to be commercial and financial. Secondly, it left a lasting legacy in the minds of Argentinians and deepened their suspicion and antagonism with regard to Britain's imperialist intentions in a way which still strongly influences their perception of British involvement in the region.

The countries of Latin America managed to win their independence from Spain in the early nineteenth century. In 1811 the Spanish formally abandoned the Falkland Islands. No other country claimed them, and the new government of the United Provinces of the Rio de la Plata (including Argentina) were too involved in the early problems of independence to do anything about them. In 1820 this government, anxious to secure all territory previously controlled by the Spanish viceroyalty, sent a ship to the Falkland Islands under Captain Jewitt to take possession. Again no protest or interest was shown by the British. In 1824 Louis Vernet was given the concession by the Buenos Aires government to develop the island of Soledad (East Falkland) and four years later it charged him with the task of establishing a colony. Although Vernet was depicted as something of a freebooter by the United States, Goebel claims he was 'by no means (an) uncultivated barbarian'. He played an important part in developing the islands, especially in the sphere of fishery conservation. On 30 August 1829 he was formally installed as governor by the Buenos Aires government, which used the occasion to lay claim to the islands and Tierra del Fuego on the basis of prior occupation, the consent of the maritime powers and geographical proximity.

British Takeover

At this time various prominent figures in Britain were urging the Foreign Office that the islands be colonized. The rationale was that possession of the Falklands would strengthen British sea power and provide a base for whaling and the suppression of piracy. In addition, the growing trade with Australia via the Straits of Magellan would make such a colony advantageous. Britain's interest grew at a time when it was seeking to dominate the seas and world trade.

However, it was the United States which put an end to Argentine control of the islands. Vernet had sought to restrict cattle killing and whaling in order to build up herds and fishing grounds for the local economy. When three US seal fishing ships persistently ignored these restrictions, Vernet seized them and accompanied one of them to the mainland for trial.

Having no formal diplomatic relations with Buenos Aires, the affairs of the United States were handled by its honorary consul George Slacum, a man of little tact or judgement. Outraged by Vernet's treatment of the American vessels, and the indifference of the mainland government to his letters of protest, Slacum engineered the sacking of the island by naval forces from the *USS Lexington.*

There was a good deal of collusion between Slacum and local British diplomats, who upheld Britain's claim to the islands. This was further reinforced when Francis Baylies, dispatched to Buenos Aires as *chargé d'affaires* by President Jackson, was given no assurances that US fishing rights would be inviolable. Baylies turned to the British envoy, Fox, urging Britain, if it exercised sovereignty, to take action against Vernet for interfering with American commerce.

Assured now that the US would not support Argentina, Britain sent two warships, the *Clio* and the *Tyne*, to the islands. A British force was landed and the Argentine flag struck on 3 January 1833. Divided by civil war and impoverished, Argentina lacked the means and power to challenge the British occupation.

Since 1833, Argentina has consistently articulated its claims to the island, yet lacked the power to back them up. In many of the treaties signed by the Argentine Republic, reservations were inserted which reiterated the claim and made allowances for restitution of the islands.

The British position has not been so solid over the years. As stated earlier in this section, already by 1910 the Foreign Office was voicing doubts as to the validity of its sovereignty claim. This remained the position until February 1936 when George Fitzmaurice, a legal advisor to the Foreign Office, wrote a briefing paper. In it he acknowledged the weakness of Britain's case as the reason why it had never been submitted for international arbitration. He encouraged the Foreign Office to attempt a new line of agreement to justify the British claim. It rested on asserting that continuous peaceful occupation of the islands entitled Britain to sovereignty. This came to be known as the 'prescription' argument, one which the British government continues to espouse.

But even this argument has proved somewhat tentative. John Troutbeck, head of the American department of the Foreign Office in 1936, stated that it was impossible to explain Britain's possession other than in terms of the most arbitrary type of seizure. Leaseback arrangements (as with Hong Kong) were suggested by the British diplomat, Sir Neville Henderson, in the 1930s, and taken up by Lord Willingdon in 1940, after he led a delegation to Buenos Aires. The Foreign Office file entitled 'Proposed offer by His Majesty's Government to reunite Falkland Islands with Argentina and acceptance of lease' (1940) is officially closed until the year 2015, but its very title indicates a serious consideration of the Argentine claim.

Thus, until the 1940s and the wholesale adoption of the 'prescription' argument, there appeared to be very little basis for Britain asserting its claim other than that arising from the relations of power between Britain and Argentina which had continued in Britain's favour since the early nineteenth century. Since power had been the main determinant of British occupation of the islands, there was little room for arguments resting on questions of 'morality' or irrefutable legal rights. The history of the British claim is rooted in its imperialist past, in the days when superior seapower enabled Britannia to rule the waves. In continuing to assert its claim, the British government is extending the life of its past imperial conquests. Maintaining its control of the islands is therefore an anachronism it can ill afford.

3 Twenty years of Talking

'Unless sovereignty is seriously negotiated and ceded in the long term, we are likely to end up in a state of armed conflict with Argentina'.
Lord Chalfont, Minister of State at the Foreign Office, 1968.

'The Falkland Islanders have to face the unpleasant fact that Britain is no longer a world power and that the rest of the world is unlikely to come to their rescue. If they are to stay where they are in the next century, it can only be on the basis of an arrangement with their South American neighbours'.
The Times 29 March 1982.

For most people in Britain, the Argentine invasion of the Falkland Islands on 2 April 1982 came as a rude awakening. It seemed inconceivable that Argentina should take such precipitate action over what is apparently a minor issue for Britain. Few British people had ever heard of the Falklands, precisely because they do not represent a vital strategic or economic interest for the country. They were hard put to see why a negotiated resolution of the conflict of interests could not have been achieved rather than resorting to a full scale military invasion.

Yet for Argentina, recuperation of the Malvinas has been a point of national pride for generations. Every Argentinian school child learns of how the British 'pirates' forcibly evicted his country from the islands in 1833. Successive governments have pressed the Argentine claim at the United Nations, the Organisation of American States and in bilateral negotiations with Britain. These negotiations have been punctuated by a series of diplomatic incidents, military encounters and warnings of invasion. Faced with the refusal by the Falkland Islanders themselves to contemplate any change in their status, Britain

United Nations Resolution 2065 (XX)
Question of the Falkland Islands (Malvinas)

The General Assembly,

Having examined the question of the Falkland Islands (Malvinas),

Taking into account the chapters of the reports of the Special Committee on the Situation with regard to the Implementation of the Declaration on the Granting of Independence to Colonial Countries and Peoples relating to the Falkland Islands (Malvinas), and in particular the conclusions and recommendations adopted by the Committee with reference to that Territory,

Considering that its resolution 1514 (XV) of 14 December 1960 was prompted by the cherished aim of bringing to an end everywhere colonialism in all its forms, one of which covers the case of the Falkland Islands (Malvinas),

Noting the existence of a dispute between the Governments of Argentina and the United Kingdom of Great Britain and Northern Ireland concerning sovereignty over the said Islands,

1. *Invites* the Governments of Argentina and the United Kingdom of Great Britain and Northern Ireland to proceed without delay with the negotiations recommended by the Special Committee on the Situation with regard to the Implementation of the Declaration on the Granting of Independence to Colonial Countries and Peoples with a view to finding a peaceful solution to the problem, bearing in mind the provisions and objectives of the Charter of the United Nations and of General Assembly resolution 1514 (XV) and the interests of the population of the Falkland Islands (Malvinas):

2. *Requests* the two Governments to report to the Special Committee and to the General Assembly at its twenty-first session on the results of the negotiations.

1398th plenary meeting,
16 December 1965.

has engaged in the sort of 'diplomatic footdragging' that has enraged and frustrated their Argentine counterparts. And on the rare occasions when progress was being made, proposals to resolve the matter have floundered in Westminster. On each occasion they have been defeated by an 'unholy alliance' of MPs on the left, who hold paramount the rights of the islanders to self-determination, and MPs on the right who point to the legal legitimacy of Britain's claim in their efforts to rekindle the last embers of empire.

In September 1964, Argentina formally reasserted its claim to the Falklands before the United Nations Committee on Decolonization. Although Britain disputed the competence of this committee to decide the issue (since it was a territorial rather than a colonial dispute), the following year the UN General Assembly adopted Resolution 2065 (XX) which invited Britain and Argentina to enter into negotiations to obtain a peaceful settlement of their differences. The adoption of this resolution was a victory for Argentina. Not only did the resolution affirm that the dispute was in fact based on a colonial claim, but it also refused to accept the British argument that the wishes of the islanders should be paramount in any negotiations. It simply urged that their 'interests' be safeguarded in whatever sovereignty agreement was reached.

Following the UN resolution, talks were started when Labour's Foreign Secretary Michael Stewart visited Buenos Aires in early 1966. However, he consistently refused to discuss the question of sovereignty and reasserted the view that the wishes of the islanders were paramount. Confronted by this hard line, Argentine feelings ran high. A small group of nationalists mounted 'Operation Condor', a symbolic invasion of the islands aboard a hijacked DC-4 airliner which they landed on the Port Stanley race course. Britain's reaction was to despatch *HMS Puma* while negotiations with the 'invaders' took place. Meanwhile an armed crowd attacked the house in which the Duke of Edinburgh was residing while in Argentina on a state visit. The Duke was unhurt, and in a speech at the end of his visit he commented: 'The factors and issues on which we agree and which bind us together are far greater and more important than these *passing ruffles* which may divide us'.

These incidents obviously had their effect, however, and by early 1968 Argentina announced that talks had reached an advanced stage. So concerned were the islanders themselves at what they considered a sell-out to Argentina that members of the islands' Executive Council wrote to MPs at Westminster denouncing the negotiations. Lord Chalfont, Minister of State at the Foreign Office who was in charge of negotiations, was clearly in favour of a settlement. He is closely associated with the Hispanic and Luso-Brazilian Council (Canning House) which seeks to encourage British firms to invest in Latin America. Obviously, the continuing Falklands dispute was hindering British capital's access to Latin America. However, Chalfont did not have the support of the British parliament, and he caused a political storm when he suggested that the sentiments expressed in the UN resolution might take precedence over the wishes of the islanders. The response was such that the Foreign Secretary was forced to reaffirm that sovereignty over the islands would not be transferred to Argentina without the islanders' approval.

Economic Rapprochement

From 1968 to 1977, negotiations concentrated on the possibility of economic cooperation with Argentina in the Falkland Islands. Although Argentina consistently argued that joint plans for the economic development of the islands were inextricably bound up with the sovereignty issue, it appeared to adopt a new approach to the problem. Moving away from attempts to isolate the islands from the mainland and thereby make their economic survival more precarious, Buenos Aires began a 'hearts and minds' campaign of economic assistance to win the islanders' support. This new policy was given obvious encouragement by the British Foreign Office. It was clear that no change in the sovereignty of the Falklands would be approved by the British parliament against the wishes of the islanders. The 'unholy alliance' of the right and left was growing in strength, by now actively encouraged by an Emergency Committee set up in London by those with interests in the islands. The main motivation for this lobbying committee came from the Falkland Island Company, in whose London offices the Committee convened and whose London manager, Mr Frank Mitchell, was its first secretary.

In November 1968, Lord Chalfont visited the Falklands and persuaded the islanders to accept an 'agreed position' with Argentina. This involved the negotiation of improved communications links with the mainland and a re-evaluation of the more fundamental issues in four to eight years' time. To the British government it was certain that the political uncertainty surrounding the colony could not continue, for, as *The Times* pointed out, 'uncertainty means the inevitable run down of the colony'. For its part, the Argentine government felt that the beneficial effects that the islanders would derive from economic cooperation could 'easily produce a fundamental change of attitudes, perhaps in ten years'. The islanders were at first wary of closer contact with the mainland, fearing that it might be the first step on a slippery slope. However, they eventually recognized that it would be in their own economic interest to be more accommodating to Argentina. As one islander said at the time, 'it would cheapen many things of daily life'.

If the islanders needed any more persuasion of where their best interests lay, it was provided by none other than the Falkland Island Company. Having recently been taken over by a subsidiary of the Slater Walker empire, and faced with declining profits from its wool trade, it announced that from the end of 1971 its packet steamer *RMS Darwin* would cease to operate from Port Stanley to Montevideo. This would have left the islands without any regular contact with the outside world.

A Preview of Crisis

'If the problem of the Falkland-Malvinas Islands leads to tragedy, the disaster will be a prime instance of the effects of non-communication all round; of a national dilemma rendered lethal by separate and total ignorance from which the political neuroses of the parties prevent escape. The combination of ignorance, patriotism, and devotion to the dogma of self-determination on the part of the British is perhaps more dangerous than Argentine legal pendantry and nationalist zealotry, because the British government has no political support in its community for resolving the conflict and the government is too frightened or complacent to give the British public a lead.

H.S. Ferns, *Argentina*, Praeger, New York 1969.

In the so-called Communications Agreements, arrived at as a result of Chalfont's diplomacy and signed in 1971 and 1972, Argentina agreed to provide a weekly air service to the islands, to simplify administrative practices so that postal, telegraph, telephone and customs services for the islanders could be streamlined, and agreed to cooperate in providing health and educational services and agricultural assistance. The air service was inaugurated in January 1972 and Argentina subsequently spent £600,000 to build a temporary airstrip capable of accommodating larger planes while a permanent airport was under construction. A further agreement was reached in 1974 when Argentina contracted to supply the islands with certain fuel products and to construct an unloading jetty and oil storage facility in Port Stanley.

However, the Argentine 'offensive of smiles' soon turned sour as Britain was accused of continuing to stall on the vital sovereignty negotiations. In August 1973 Argentina complained that Britain had virtually paralysed negotiations over the Falklands and that Buenos Aires would have to reappraise its options. This was after Argentina had spent considerable sums on health, education and transport services for the islands. Matters came to a head in December 1974 when Argentina learnt that Britain was granting oil exploration concessions for offshore drilling around the islands. Argentina said she would refuse to recognize the concessions and threatened to take the islands by force. The British ambassador's residence in Buenos Aires was attacked and it looked as if relations had reached a new low.

Matters worsened still further during the following year. The British government announced that an economic and social survey of the

Falklands was to be undertaken by Lord Shackleton, whose father the famous Antarctic explorer is buried on South Georgia. Argentina insisted that the mission was not welcome in the uncertain atmosphere of the time, and in January 1976 called for Britain to withdraw its ambassador from Buenos Aires until such time as it was prepared to negotiate the issue of sovereignty over the Falkland Islands. The following day the British Cultural Institute in Cordoba was destroyed by a bomb and, as the Shackleton mission was about to leave the Falklands in early February, an Argentine warship fired across the bows of a British research vessel.

This worsening state of affairs persuaded the British government that the sovereignty issue had to be confronted. In response to the *Shackleton Report*, it was clear (as Mr Anthony Crosland, the Labour government's Foreign Secretary, pointed out in early 1977) that the economic development of the Falkland Islands could only take place within the 'framework of greater political and economic cooperation in the region as a whole'. Mr Ted Rowlands, Minister of State at the Foreign Office, visited the islands and made it clear in talks with the Argentine government that sovereignty was to be discussed. But by July 1977, the talks had not progressed and British parliamentary pressure was running high. One hundred and forty MPs of all parties signed a motion demanding that Britain should retain sovereignty over the islands in accordance with the islanders' wishes. Once again Argentina found its efforts thwarted and its angry reactions persuaded the Callaghan government to send *HMS Phoebe, HMS Alacrity* and the nuclear submarine *HMS Dreadnought* to the South Atlantic to discourage an imminent Argentine invasion.

Negotiations continued irregularly throughout 1978 and 1979 but in late 1980 the new Conservative government announced another initiative. Mr Nicholas Ridley, Minister of State at the Foreign Office, visited the Falklands to consult the islanders about their future. Various proposals were presented to them: the transfer of sovereignty to Argentina and a leaseback arrangement, whereby Britain would continue to administer and govern the islands during the leaseback period, (perhaps 99 years) despite sovereignty having passed to Argentina, the freezing of negotiations for a period, or the breaking off of negotiations altogether. As he stated in the House of Commons on 2 December 1980:

The essential elements of any solution would be that it should preserve the British administration, law and way of life for the islanders, while releasing the potential of the islands' economy and of their maritime resources, at present blighted by the dispute.

He made it clear that Argentina was getting impatient and that the time to find an agreeable solution was running out. However, the same 'unholy alliance' of left and right wing MPs united as they had done in the past and brought his efforts to nothing. The islanders eventually decided on a 25-year freeze on sovereignty negotiations and this was communicated to Argentina in early 1981.

Relations received a setback later in the same year when Britain warned that she would take action against any company drilling for oil in Argentina's most recent concession area, Magallenes Este. This area comes within 96 miles of the Falklands and crosses the putative median line between the mainland and the islands. For its part, Argentina also complained at the attempts of the Falkland Island Committee (the successor to the Emergency Committee set up to lobby Parliament in 1968) to halt the islands' population decline by transferring families to the Falklands from St Helena, a small South Atlantic island, colonized by Britain, with a population of 5,000 people. They argued that this action disturbed the *status quo* at a time when delicate negotiations were under way.

The Final Touches

By late 1981, Argentine hopes that Britain was rethinking its Falkland policy were fuelled by two separate developments. In October, the British government refused to give the Falkland Islanders exemption from the Nationality Bill then before Parliament. This meant that about one third of the islanders no longer had the right to live in Britain, a proportion that would increase as time passed, and fewer of them would be able to fulfill the Bill's requirements for residence. A few months earlier, in announcing the cuts in the naval budget in order to meet the costs of the Trident missile programme, the Ministry of Defence confirmed that *HMS Endurance*, the only British naval presence in the South Atlantic, was to be scrapped. Argentina surmised that Britain was effectively pulling out of the South Atlantic.

But in early 1982, Argentina's hopes were again dashed. Following talks in New York, Argentina announced that it would put an end to negotiations and seek a procedure which better suited its interests if solutions were not found. It demanded monthly meetings until the issue was resolved. The situation had become critical. In February, President Galtieri was reported to have secured a commitment to neutrality in his meeting with Uruguʳan President Gregorio Alvarez, should Argentina decide on militarʸ action. This was crucial given that Montevideo could have been an ideal staging post for the British fleet. Further evidence that something dramatic was about to break came from an article written in *La Prensa* in Buenos Aires by a senior

Argentine political commentator, Iglesies Rouco. He stated clearly that 'this year Buenos Aires will recover the islands by force' and that in the new initiatives that were about to be launched 'military action was not excluded from consideration'.

The stage was therefore set. All that was needed was a spark to transform what was for Britain a nagging diplomatic irritant into its biggest political and military crisis for a generation. That spark was provided by Constantino Davidoff.

South Georgia had until the early 1960s been the base for the world's largest on-shore whaling industry. The advent of factory ships, which processed whale carcasses at sea, made shore-based facilities obsolete. Davidoff's Islas Georgia Company had contracts to demolish for scrap three whaling stations located at Leith Harbour, Stromness and Husvik. According to documents in his possession, stamped with a round seal which reads 'Received by the British Embassy', he had the full permission of the British Consul to land on South Georgia.

Unfortunately, when they arrived on 19 March, his men raised the blue and white Argentine flag. What Davidoff claims was no more than a patriotic gesture was interpreted by members of a nearby British research team as something more sinister. They radioed London and warned that a possible Argentine invasion was underway. Britain protested to Argentina and *HMS Endurance* was dispatched with a party of marines. Argentina replied that as Davidoff's party was on Argentine soil, it should be protected against forcible removal and sent units of its navy to the area. The first act of the tragedy was about to begin.

45

Argentina

○ National capital   ━━━━━ International boundary
○ Town   ············· Department boundary

Kilometres
0 100 200 300 400 500

BOLIVIA

PARAGUAY

BRAZIL

ANDES

JUJUY

SALTA

FORMOSA

TUCU-MAN

○ S. Miguel de Tucuman

CHACO

CATAMARCA

SANTIAGO DEL ESTERO

MISIONES

CORRIENTES

LA RIOJA

SANTA FE

SAN JUAN

Cordoba ○

CHILE

Santa Fe ○

ENTRE RIOS

SANTIAGO

CORDOBA

Rosario ○

URUGUAY

Mendoza ○

SAN LUIS

MONTEVIDEO ○

MENDOZA

BUENOS AIRES ○
La Plata ○

BUENOS AIRES

LA PAMPA

NEUQUEN

Bahia Blanca ○

Mar del Plata ○

RIO NEGRO

SOUTH PACIFIC OCEAN

ANDES

SOUTH ATLANTIC OCEAN

CHUBUT

Comodoro Rivadavia ○

SANTA CRUZ

ISLAS MALVINAS/
FALKLAND ISLANDS
Stanley

TIERRA DEL FUEGO
Ushuaia

Argentina In Brief

Area (mainland)	1,072,072 sq. miles (UK = 94,000 sq. miles)
Population	Total 27.7 millions (1980) Growth rate 1.6% per year Urban 85.7% (1980)
Principal towns (1980)	Greater Buenos Aires 9,927,404 Greater Córdoba 982,018 Rosário 954,606 Mendoza 596,796
The people	Origins Mainly European. 40% of the population of Buenos Aires is of Italian descent. Language Spanish Religion Roman Catholic (94.3%)
Economy (1980)	GDP Total US$56.6 billion Per capita US$1,935 Trade Exports US$ 8.0 billion Imports US$10.0 billion Principal exports: Grains and other agricultural products 51.5%. Meat and meat products 22.7%. Manufactured goods 25.8%. Foreign debt 1978 US$ 7.8 billion 1979 US$11.3 billion 1980 US$14.0 billion Debt service 1978 US$ 2.2 billion payments 1979 US$ 1.8 billion 1980 US$ 2.8 billion 1981 US$ 3.6 billion (est).
Wealth distribution	70% of land is owned by 1% of population. 65% of industrial production is controlled by 0.2% of producers, who employ 50% of the labour force.

Sources: Inter American Development Bank; British Argentina Campaign; Ministry of Economy, Treasury and Finance, Argentina; National Institute of Statistics and Census (INDEC), Argentina.

47

Political Parties

The activities of the following parties were 'suspended' in March 1976.

Partido Justicialista (Peronist Party)
The largest Argentine party. Created by Juan Domingo Perón in the late 1940s, it has developed more as a movement than as a coherent political organization. Perón managed to unify several different currents of opinion, from neo-marxists to the extreme right wing within the same structures. Thanks to demagogic and populist policies, Perón obtained support from the working class and middle class sectors of the country to develop a nationalistic programme during his first two periods as president (1947 to 1955). Re-elected once more as president in 1973, he failed to control the different groups of his own political supporters and after his death in July 1974 the movement split into several factions. There are now attempts to reunify the organization but no leader skilful enough to achieve this has so far emerged. The main differences lie between the 'political sector' which represents the interests of local industrialists and controls the structures of the party, and the powerful 'trade union sector' which has the capacity to mobilize the party's popular base. In 1981 and 1982 a new 'social democratic' sector has emerged known as 'Intransigent Peronism' which seems to be obtaining support from left-wing Peronists and some trade unionists.

Union Civica Radical (Radical Party)
The second largest political party. Formed at the end of last century, it attracted the support of European immigrants, medium and small-scale farmers and emerging industrialist class. It now represents the middle sectors of society. Its programme is very similar to the Peronist one but it has less mass support than the Peronist Party. The Radical Party has an internal organizational structure closely modelled on European counterparts. Over the past few years it split into different tendencies, now regrouped along two 'lines': the traditionalists and the reformists.

Partido Intransigente (Intransigent Party)
Originally splitting from the Radical Party in the late 1950s, this organization has developed as a centre-left alternative. It mainly represents professionals, small businessmen and students. Its leaders have been attending conferences of the Socialist International.

Movimiento de Integracion y Desarrollo (MID)
An organization without mass support but with strong links to big business and the multinationals. In elections it has always been allied with the Peronists, although it originally formed part of the Radical Party. Its programme includes the creation of big state monopolies as well as the opening of the economy to some multinationals on the basis of 'fair' competition. Its leadership has been defined as 'opportunist technocrats' ready to join any electoral coalition with popular organizations.

Movimiento Cristiano Democratico (Christian Democratic Movement)
Despite the power of the Catholic church, Argentina never developed a powerful Christian Democratic Party. In the late 1970s a group of centre-right Catholic organizations initiated discussions on the formation of such a party. Two of the main forces behind this project are the small Partido Demócrata Progresista (PDP), and the Partido Popular Cristiano (PPC), which has closer links with liberals in the church.

Movimiento Socialista (Socialist Movement)
In the same way as the Christian Democrats, a group of small traditional socialist parties — linked to the Socialist International — have been working together to form a united socialist party. The main organizations in this coalition are the Partido Socialista Popular (PSP, the official representative of the Socialist International); the Confederación Socialista (led by 96-year-old Alicia Moreau de Justo, widow of the founder of the first Socialist Party in Argentina); and the Partido Socialista Unificado (PSU). Their supporters are mainly urban intellectuals.

Alianza Federalista (Federalist Alliance)
A group of small conservative parties combined under this name in the 1973 elections and gained third place. Over the past few years the alliance has collapsed and most of the parties within it supported the dictatorship.

Partido Comunista Argentino (Argentine Communist Party)
Founded in 1918, this is a traditional pro-Soviet communist party. It organized the General Confederation of Workers in the 1930s, but lost control of it when the Peronists took over the organization. Today it has a powerful national structure based on support from intellectuals, students, artists and a small percentage of workers. Its programme

foresees a Government of National Unity formed by civilians and the military.

The following parties were declared 'prohibited' in March 1976.

Partido Montonero (Montoneros)
Created in 1969 by a group of Catholic and nationalist students, this armed organization grew rapidly within the Peronist movement. In the early 1970s the Montoneros controlled the Peronist youth organizations and developed a vast national political and military structure. One of the major targets for repression after the coup in 1976, it no longer has any influential organization inside the country and its leadership and militants live in exile. It has been weakened by several divisions over the past few years, but all its factions share a strategy of popular war based on Peronist ideas.

Partido Revolucionario de los Trabajadores (Revolutionary Workers' Party)
Created by Trotskyists in 1965, this Marxist-Leninist party became known due to the actions of its military front, the Peoples Revolutionary Army (ERP), the second largest armed organization in the 1970s and a major target of repression by the armed forces. Despite some spectacular rural and urban guerrilla operations, their lack of working class support isolated them from the mass struggles of the Argentinian people. Formed mainly by intellectuals, students and some workers, it now has few supporters inside the country, and its leadership and members — after several splits — live in exile, no longer identifying themselves with a Trotskyist position.

Partido Socialista de los Trabajadores (Socialist Workers' Party)
The major Trotskyist organization in the country. Although a victim of the repression, it has grown during recent years and now operates semi-legally. It was first created in 1972 after the union of three small Trotskyist parties.

Partido Comunista Revolucionario (Revolutionary Communist Party)
Split from the Communist Party in the 1960s criticizing its reformist policies. For some years it debated various radical strategies, and in 1973 became a Maoist organization, supporting the Peronist regime.

Other left-wing organizations of indeterminate strength include the Partido Comunista Marxista Leninista, the Politica Obrera, the Poder Obrero, and the Peronismo de Base.

4 Argentina: Foreign Control and Nationalism

'Without saying so in as many words, which would be tactless, what I really mean is that Argentina must be regarded as an essential part of the British Empire. We cannot get on without her, nor she without us'.
Sir Malcolm Robertson, British Ambassador to Argentina, 1929.

Introduction

The depth of nationalistic feeling over the Malvinas and the view held almost universally in Argentina that the Falklands war was a struggle against British imperialism, can only be understood in the context of Britain's historic relations with Argentina. In fact the history of Argentina since its independence from Spain cannot be told without constant reference to the part played by British interests in the country. It is no exaggeration to say that the economic and social structure of modern Argentina took shape in the decades before 1914 when British influence was at its height. The irony, from the perspective of 1982, is that while the issue of the Falkland Islands lay just below the surface of Anglo-Argentine relations after the 1830s, the seeds of Argentine nationalism were sown by the very nature of Britain's contacts with the country.

The image of Argentina as flat, fertile pampas criss-crossed by British-owned railway lines, a nation growing prosperous on the export of wheat and beef to feed hungry Britain, financed by British capital, and prizing the closeness of Anglo-Argentine relations, is merely one side of the coin. The other is of one of the largest cities in the world, whose inhabitants were predominantly poor Italian and Spanish immigrants and who had little share in the highly profitable

51

nexus of Argentine land and British capital. To a growing extent in the twentieth century, the British connection came to be resented as an intrusion which distorted Argentine development towards a vulnerable dependence on agricultural activities and away from the growth of manufacturing industry. This resentment grew as Britain's own economic decline made it impossible for her to sustain the role of mother-country to her unofficial Dominion, while it increased her reluctance to give up the advantages of her special relationship with Argentina.

The Establishment of Argentina

Early British Interests

The early independence period in Argentina was a time of confusion and instability, and not until the 1820s, with the influence of Rivadavia, was order restored from chaos. In 1824 Buenos Aires contracted a loan of £1 million in London (of which little more than half reached Argentina), but in common with all the borrowings made by the former Spanish colonies at this time the loan went quickly into default. The reasons were straightforward. It had been promoted in London on the basis of the premiums to be secured, rather than on Argentina's financial capacity to service it. In practice the primitive economic structure of Argentina, based at this time on the exploitation of wild cattle herds, was incapable of supporting the foreign loan, which remained in default until the 1850s.

The British connection with Argentina was slow to develop. By 1824 there were 3,000 Britons settled in the country. Some owned land, others were employed in the commercial community, but most had little capital. Nonetheless by mid-century the British community numbered nearer 30,000, and had acquired an economic significance far exceeding that of any other national group in the young republic. British manufactured goods, especially textiles, dominated the import trade into the River Plate, while British shipping monopolized the carrying trades of the region.

The Era of Rosas

The second quarter of the nineteenth century was not in fact an easy period for foreign interests in Argentina. After the fall of the liberal, European-influenced, Rivadavia in 1828, Argentina was ruled by the *caudillo* landowner Rosas, who elevated traditional *gaucho* skills with a sharp knife into a system of personal power based on terror. The Foreign Office in London was uncertain of its attitude: Rosas was uncivilized, and gave no welcome to British capital, but he at least kept the country in order, and established British interests and commerce continued to grow, if slowly. Rosas himself was eventually ousted by rival landowners, frustrated by the limitations of his political and economic system, in 1852. The dictator found exile in England, near Southampton, where he lived for twenty-five years and now lies buried.

Britain and Liberal Argentina 1862-1913

The fall of Rosas was a major turning point in the development of Argentina, though the changes were neither immediate nor total. For a decade traditional antagonisms between Buenos Aires and the rest of Argentina delayed the adoption of the new liberalism. More seriously, Rivadavia's vision in the 1820s of state lands to attract immigrants was defeated by the consolidation under Rosas of a small class of vast landowners. Hence, when the surge of immigration came at the end of the century it was urban and Latin rather than Anglo-Saxon and rural. But the *gaucho* style so characteristic of the Rosas era, with its suspicion of foreign capital and foreign technology, was now replaced by the assiduous pursuit of modernization and progress. In Europe, expanding populations and rising incomes meant an increasing demand for food. Argentina was well placed to meet that demand. By 1880 the hostile Indians who were the only obstacle to extended settlement of the plains had been exterminated. What was needed to make this abundant land productive was capital, which Britain now provided on a huge scale.

British Investment

Outside the Empire, only the US received a greater volume of British foreign investment. By the First World War, Britain had lent or invested £770 million in South America, of which Argentina's share was almost half. Most of the investment was in railways which were built, owned and operated by Britons: the Buenos Aires Great Southern, the Central Argentine, the Buenos Aires and Pacific, and a dozen others. British lines dominated Argentina's railway system. Capital was drawn also to land, banking (the London and River Plate Bank was founded in 1862 and was the direct ancestor of today's Lloyds Bank International), commerce, shipping services, insurance, urban utilities, and meat-packing plants. The British community in Argentina expanded greatly around these assets, and possessed a power and influence out of proportion to their numbers. Founding their own newspapers, schools, clubs, and sports, the British formed an elite group whose prestige and style all well-bred or ambitious Argentines sought to emulate.

British Trade

The association of British capital with Argentine (or Anglo-Argentine) land ownership provoked occasional frictions, but in the long run was immensely profitable for both parties. As the railways opened up new land for cultivation, land values rose, rail traffic increased, and the prosperity of the agrarian economy consolidated the dominant status of the landowning class and its British allies. By 1913 Britain was buying wheat and beef from Argentina to the value of £40 million per year, four times as much as at the turn of the century. As a market, Argentina still sought British cottons and woollens, hardware, china-ware, etc, but of growing importance in the import trade was the British companies' demand for rails, rolling stock and Cardiff coal. This was a captive market of immense importance to Britain's staple industries which elsewhere were losing ground to the industrial capacity of the US and Germany.

The Inter-War Years

The expansive phase of Anglo-Argentine relations reached their high point on the eve of the First World War. Though a special relationship persisted until after 1945, it did so on very different terms. The situation was further changed by the fact that those who had not participated in the benefits of an economic system based on agricultural production for export markets now increasingly found a political voice to express their resentment. The landowning class was one target; the 'imperialist' role of Britain in Argentine affairs was another.

Britain, the US, and Argentina

Britain's role in the international economy was much changed in the 1920s, and there were special factors in the Anglo-Argentine connection to complicate the situation. During the war the US had supplanted Britain's position as principal supplier of manufactures to Argentina and maintained this supremacy after the war. Not only were US exports available, they were also goods in growing demand. Road transport vehicles were a major category, and had the additional merit of offering competition to the British-owned trams and railways. British exports, in contrast, were still dominated by the traditional categories of textiles, railway equipment, and coal, which comprised a much reduced share of the market. This commercial shift towards dependence on the US had its financial counterpart. Although massive interest and dividend payments still flowed to Britain from existing assets in Argentina, the British economy in the

1920s no longer generated huge financial surpluses for overseas investment on the pre-war scale. New York was now the principal source of foreign loans, and foreign investment in Argentine manufacturing industry inevitably came from the US.

The logic of the situation seemed therefore to dictate that Argentina would associate increasingly with the US while the British connection withered. But Britain held a trump card which revealed the nature and extent of British power over Argentina. Simply, Argentina was an export economy, the main markets for her cereals and beef were in Europe generally and Britain in particular, and for chilled beef (the top quality product on which the prosperity of the cattle industry depended) Britain was the only market. In vain did Argentina press for access to the US market. Argentine beef was excluded at first by tariffs and then by outright prohibition on the grounds that foot-and-mouth disease was endemic to the country. Hence in the late 1920s, even before the world depression, the bilateralist slogan 'buy from those who buy from us' was current in Argentina, and it became government policy to increase its purchases from Britain in order to preserve the principal export market for beef.

The Roca-Runciman Treaty 1933

The danger the cattle industry envisaged, namely that Britain would concede the demand for preference for Empire meat producers and so restrict Argentine access to the British market, nonetheless became fact in the aftermath of the depression. Following the granting of imperial preferences in the Ottawa Agreements of 1932, Britain proceeded to conclude a bilateral trade and payments agreement, the Roca-Runciman Treaty, with Argentina in 1933. The Radical Party government of the 1920s had by then been displaced by a *coup* in 1930. The new regime, which strongly represented the large land-owners and cattle interests, secured in the Treaty a meat quota in the British market, though at a reducing level and on less favourable terms than those for Empire producers. In exchange, the regime conceded lower tariffs on British goods with special treatment for coal; favourable foreign exchange allocations to permit interest and profit remittances to London; and a promise of benevolent treatment for British enterprises (which in practice meant limiting competition from road transport systems). The Treaty was a short-term triumph for British interests and little short of a humiliation for Argentina. Its effect was to intensify nationalist sentiments, especially among intellectuals and the middle class and, rightly or wrongly, it offered an alibi for at least a generation for Argentina's perceived failure to realise its potential as a nation. When the Treaty was extended in 1936, even *The Economist* was led to question whether a further ounce of flesh would be exacted from Argentina every few years.

The Second World War

During the Second World War, through most of which Argentina preserved its neutrality, support for the Axis powers was considerable among the military and the right wing of the Conservative Party (in which, ironically, the rural sector was strongly represented). But the logic of Argentina's economic structure forced her to remain closely linked with the Allies. Britain wanted meat but could not afford to pay for it, while Argentina needed to dispose of its meat production. Thus, a new payments agreement with Britain in September 1939 meant that Argentina would accept payment into a sterling account in London which could not be used for dollar purchases and on which no interest was payable.

By the end of the war Argentina had extended free credit to Britain to the extent of £340 million. Britain was anxious that these funds should be used by the Argentine government to buy up British assets in Argentina, especially the railways — ageing, unprofitable, and about to suffer changes in their legal status. Argentina might have preferred to have all its sterling transferred into dollars, but Britain's huge post-war dollar problem ruled out the possibility. In any case, the position of the foreign-owned railways had been so long a matter of popular resentment that their acquisition in 1948, for £150 million, may be regarded as an inevitability. The repatriation of the railways was hailed as an act of economic independence from British imperialism. The liberator was Juan Perón, and a new phase in Argentine history was opening. The special relationship between Britain and Argentina had been brought to an end by a simple cash transaction.

The Rise of Perón

By the early 1940s, Argentina had a considerable industrial base, developed as a response to world depression and war. These dislocations in the international economy, of which Argentina was a highly dependent and vulnerable part, reduced the country's export earnings and capacity to import. This stimulated the creation of an industrial sector geared to the manufacture of previously imported consumer goods. By 1944 industrial production made up a larger proportion of total production than ranching, the production of cereals and agricultural raw materials, although these traditional export activities did not lose their key position in the economy.

Economic changes had important social and political implications. The old order had rested on a close alliance between the cattle ranchers — of which those who fattened the cattle for sale to the slaughter houses rather than the cattle breeders were the most important group — and British imperialism.

In the 1930s the cattle fatteners, who were still the most powerful group in the country, had accepted the move into industry and an increasingly interventionist state as a way out of the economic crisis of the depression years. But they themselves did not invest in industry. This was mostly in the hands of a national industrial class which had risen out of Argentina's large urban middle sector and immigrant population. These industrialists tended not to have any party or movement which expressed their interests politically. But as industry grew to play an increasingly important part in the economy, they came to have more defined interests of their own, not always coinciding with those of the landowning elite which controlled the state.

The development of industry also had a profound impact on the growth of the working class. Even before the rapid expansion of industry in the 1930s, Argentina had a small industrial base and a well-organised, militant working class influenced by the anarcho-syndicalist ideas brought by Italian and Spanish immigrants. The ranks of these workers were to be swelled in the 1930s by a massive influx of migrants from Argentina's rural areas. They headed mostly for Buenos Aires, attracted by the growing demand for labour in the new industries at a time when unemployment in the rural areas had reached serious levels. This movement from the countryside to the city amounted to a mass exodus. Between 1936 and 1947, the proportion of Argentines born in the provinces who moved to metropolitan Buenos Aires was equivalent to almost 40 per cent of the natural population increase of these provinces. In the same period, half a million persons entered the industrial labour force, an increase of over 100 per cent.

During the period of industrial expansion, capital was accumulated by keeping wages low and repressing the labour movement. Despite its long history and traditions, the Argentine trade union movement was weakened at this time by the competition for leadership of the movement between the socialists, communists and anarcho-syndicalists and was unable to act in united support of its demands on wages and conditions.

It was in this situation of a decline of the old alliances and the rise of new classes with distinct aspirations, that a military *coup* took place in 1943 led by General Ramirez and supported by a number of junior officers. Amongst them was Colonel Juan Perón who became the Minister of Labour in the new government.

There are many interpretations of the role of Perón in Argentine history. But there is no doubt that his impact on the labour movement was immense. During his period in the labour ministry he was able to satisfy many of the demands which the working class had been making — without success — during the 1930s and he secured a solid base amongst them. He was helped by the favourable economic circumstances during the Second World War and Korean War in which prices for Argentina's exports were very good and the country built up a high level of foreign reserves.

Between 1943 and 1948 real wages rose by 37 per cent and from 1943 to 1949 labour's share of national income rose from about 45.6 per cent to 59 per cent. Welfare laws and social security programmes significantly improved the standard of living of the working class. Perón also made a particular effort, along with his legendary wife Evita, to organize the new workers, the recent immigrants from the rural areas. However, there is evidence that he won over many of the older trade unionists as well and Perón soon gained control over the bureaucracy of the movement. The constitution of the General Confederation of Labour (CGT) was changed to proclaim that its fundamental purpose was to support Perón and his policies. Any union which tried to maintain an independent position was refused legal recognition. Fourteen major strikes were declared illegal in 1948 and a further twelve in 1949. Democracy in the unions was stifled and in this way Perón built up a powerful political base for his presidential ambitions. When Perón was challenged by the military in 1945 it was the CGT which called a strike which won his release from prison and paved the way for his victory in the 1946 presidential elections.

In the years that followed, Perón attempted to develop a project for Argentina based on national economic development and social justice, the accumulation of wealth and its distribution, with the state playing a pivotal role in the process. His concern to build national industry at the expense of the rural sector, won him the financial support of a large number of industrialists.

But growth and redistribution in an economy as dependent on external forces as Argentina's could not be sustained when world prices for its exports began to fall and export earnings suffered further from a series of droughts and bad harvests. Favourable economic circumstances had enabled Perón to pursue populist policies which gained him mass support but which did not produce sustained economic development. Even the rural sector was not seriously harmed initially by the channelling of its surplus into industry. But as earnings fell, the contradictions in the Peronist project became apparent. Further development of industry depended on imports of raw materials, fuel and machinery and would not allow for the high real wages Perón had hitherto guaranteed the labour force. Perón could either radicalize his project, introduce an agrarian reform and more sweeping nationalizations, or abandon his emphasis on national economic development and social justice, seeking capital from outside the country and squeezing the living standards of the workers.

The second part of Perón's period in office (he was re-elected in 1951) was marked by a move to the right in pursuit of this latter course. At the same time he began to strengthen political controls, increase repression and censorship, arrest independent union leaders and attempt to centralize political life under his leadership. In the process he attacked the privileges of the church and earned its active opposition to his government.

Despite this move to the right, it was the working class who still tried to defend Perón when in 1955 the rest of Argentina allied against him. In that year a *coup* supported by the majority of the army, the church, the landowners and the national industrialists overthrew him and forced him into exile.

The Military versus Peronism

The overthrow of Perón was not the end of Peronism. Its influence continued to pervade Argentine political life, although the military attempted to turn the clock back and exclude the newly mobilized and overwhelmingly Peronist workers from the political arena. The resulting tensions lay behind the endemic instability of the post-Perón years.

The economic policies of the military regime which took over in 1955 aimed at deflation, stabilization, a return to the traditional, dependent pattern of growth favouring the export sector and the search for industrial development through foreign investment. Between 1958 and 1962 this strategy was elaborated by President Frondizi, and became known as *desarrollismo* (developmentalism). Originally Frondizi had sought an alliance with Peronism. In a secret deal he promised the Peronists the right to participate in the provincial elections of 1962 in return for support in the 1958 elections. After these elections he turned from an appeal to the popular base of Peronism towards an alliance with local industrialists. But this class was weak and the landowning elite resisted attempts to channel its surplus into industry. Frondizi therefore turned to external sources of investment and opened the doors to foreign capital.

Between 1958 and 1963 US$500 million in foreign capital flowed into Argentina, of which 65 per cent was from the United States and 90 per cent of which went into the petrochemical, chemical, automobile, and electrical machinery sectors, the most dynamic branches of industry. Foreign capital increased its share of industrial production in Argentina from 20 to 28 per cent. A study by the Economic Commission for Latin America (ECLA) in 1969 which referred to the effects of post-Peronist policies noted that the 'net effect was a large shift in income in favour of profits, particularly in the agricultural sector, and the consequent rise in the degree of inequality . . . (and) can to an important extent be regarded as a return to the pre-Second World War income distribution'.

But persistent balance of payments problems and rising inflation were signs that the Argentine economy was still in trouble. At the same time the policies pursued clashed head-on with the interests of the working class. The provincial elections of 1962 in which the Peronists had participated showed they still have overwhelming support. However, while the military were resolute in their opposition to Peronism they were still deeply divided on how to contain it, whether it should be banned or coopted.

By 1966 one military officer had secured sufficient support within the armed forces to be recognised as undisputed military leader: he was General Juan Carlos Onganía. Onganía became president after a *coup* in that year and initiated a process which has been compared to the military 'revolution' in Brazil in 1964. It involved doing away with political parties and elections. Social and political order were to be imposed by force so as to pursue a programme of economic modernization. This was to be based on the restructuring of the economy to favour the expansion of large-scale monopoly industries linked to foreign capital whose confidence in the country would be restored by firm military rule. US investment in Argentina had indeed increased from US$800 million in 1962 to US$1.5 billion in 1968 reaching US$2.6 billion by the end of 1976. Between 1963 and 1977, 53 Argentine companies were bought out by foreign firms. A total of 19 local banks were sold to foreign interests between 1967 and 1969. By 1970 foreign banks held 40.5 per cent of the total commercial deposits in Argentine private banks. By 1976 this had risen to 58 per cent.

The Onganía programme also included a wage freeze and a ban on strikes. But the Argentine working class could not be so easily neutralized. In 1969 they fought back with a vengeance. Their economic and political grievances culminated in a series of popular uprisings in that year, beginning in Córdoba (the *Cordobazo*) but spreading to the other main industrial centres. These semi-insurrections profoundly shook Argentina's ruling elite, particularly as they were led by a more militant workers' leadership which rejected the willingness of a sector of the Peronist trade union bureaucracy to collaborate with the military. This time the workers' movement was supported by a large section of a disaffected middle class. Small and medium-sized businesses had been adversely affected by the government's support for large scale enterprises, while other professional and student groups reacted strongly against what they saw as the denationalization of the economy. Students in particular joined with workers on the streets of Argentina's main industrial towns. Together they paved the way for the fall of the Onganía government in 1970.

But more than this, the workers' mobilizations, which continued into the early 1970s, forced the military to appreciate that some deal had to be done with Peronism in order to restore stability to the country. It was President Lanusse, a strong anti-Peronist, who in 1971 began talks with the Peronists. His aim was to integrate the movement preferably without Perón himself, and secure support for his own presidential ambitions.

From the point of view of the Argentine ruling elite, Perón had become the only figure capable of defusing the increasingly radical demands of the workers by channelling them into some populist solution which nevertheless would, as in Perón's earlier period in office, retain existing socio-economic structures. In 1973 a US State Department official quoted by the North American Council for Latin America (NACLA) in the *Hour of the Furnaces*, summed up this view: 'I think this is the moment for Perón. He alone can bring cohesion to Argentina. There is no one else left. So he has come to represent opportunity'.

The Return of Perón

Elections were held in Argentina in March 1973 and Perón's representative Hector Cámpora, was elected with nearly 50 per cent of the vote. Perón himself returned to Argentina later that year and in presidential elections in September won the support of 62 per cent of the electorate.

The expectations on Perón's return varied greatly. A number of armed guerrilla organizations had emerged in Argentina by this time of which the largest, the *Montoneros*, was within the Peronist movement. The *Montoneros* had their origins within nationalism and Catholicism, and amongst disillusioned members of the traditional left as well as Peronism itself. For them, Perón represented a nationalist and socialist option for Argentina and they believed that

61

through a prolonged war against imperialism and the local oligarchy Argentina could leap the phase of 'parliamentary democracy' and reach socialism with a nationalist flavour, linked to the masses via Peronism. Such a programme of nationalist reconstruction was not totally incompatible with Perón's project on his return, but the *Montoneros'* capacity for mass mobilization in support of its more radical aims certainly was.

While the *Montoneros* represented the main current on the left of Peronism at this time, the right wing of the movement had a totally different view of the purpose of Perón's return, stressing the nationalist and populist roots of Peronism rather than socialism. A document issued by this wing of the movement stated the following: 'Justicialism (the name adopted by the Peronist movement) was born as a Third Position between capitalism and the different schools of dogmatic socialism, such as communism, scientific socialism, state socialism etc . . . When Perón speaks of national socialism, he is referring exclusively to the change which attempts to transform the community of wage earners into a community of entrepreneurs so that all the people and not just a privileged minority, may enjoy the benefits of production and profit. This clarification of the difference between dogmatic socialism and national socialism is not only fitting, but necessary, because in these times of stormy waters, fishermen are working feverishly with their red nets'.

In addition to the increasingly violent conflicts between the two main wings of Peronism, there were other non-Peronist forces in Argentina to be considered. The second large party according to 1973 elections was the Radical Party (UCR) the traditional party of the middle class led by Ricardo Balbín and it was willing to enter into discussions with Perón. The small Communist Party had supported an alliance which failed to challenge Perón's candidacy and was later prepared to make concessions to Peronism. On the left of the spectrum there were the other armed organisations outside the Peronist movement, most notably the Popular Revolutionary Army (ERP) which continued its operations against foreign corporations and military targets after the return of Perón, offering him only a temporary truce if the organization was not persecuted.

Perón's own programme of National Reconstruction involved the encouragement of industrial exports, attempts to 'regulate' foreign investment and to seek such investment from countries other than the United States, a policy of favouring local over foreign capital and the opening up of trade and diplomatic relationships with Communist and Third World countries. Its initial phase involved a stabilization plan based on a Social Pact between the CGT and the organization representing the interests of small and medium-sized businesses, the

CGE. In return for a promise of price stability from the CGE and of basic structural reforms from the government, the CGT pledged not to strike for two years and to agree to a two year wage freeze after an initial 20 per cent rise. The measures were partly to reduce inflationary pressures at a time when inflation was already at dangerous levels and real wages had fallen during 1972 to one of the lowest levels in the past decade. It was very much within the Peronist tradition of inter-class cooperation in the distribution of income between wage-earners and business interests mediated by the state.

Once again, Perón was initially favoured by the propitious external conditions in 1973, when the value of Argentina's exports rose 65 per cent higher than in 1972. This enabled the government to pursue an expansionary policy which doubled the real rate of growth in 1973. But by the end of the year the international situation was reversed following the oil price hikes, and the terms of trade fell by over 20 per cent. This, together with the internal expansionary policies, began to create the first strains in the economy which were to build up in the following years. In addition, the workers' movement was in no mood to accept the Social Pact negotiated by their leaders. In the second half of 1973 they went on the offensive with a wave of strikes which was not only around wages and conditions but also involved demands for union democracy by the rank and file against the corrupt union leadership.

The *Montoneros* through the Peronist Workers Youth (JTP) movement as well as the leaders of the trade union movement who had led the *Cordobazo* played an important role in the mobilization of the working class. But they still called for support for Perón and his policies as 'the only possibility to achieve national liberation'. This became increasingly difficult to sustain as Perón himself began to denounce the left of the movement as 'infiltrators' and 'foreign mercenaries', although initially they blamed this not on Perón but on the reactionary elements within his government. Perón however moved increasingly against the radical wing of the movement. A Law of Professional Associations gave the union bureaucracies the right to intervene in their regional bodies to overthrow combative leaders.

A Law of Redundancy enabled the university to dismiss 'excess personnel', which in effect meant the more radical staff. A Law of Compulsory Arbitration more or less outlawed the right to strike. Then Perón moved against some of the left-wing provincial governors through the Act of Obligation to National Security which gave the federal government the right to intervene in the internal affairs of the provinces in the interest of 'national security'. Nor was Perón's gradual reformist programme compatible with the move to socialism which the left of the movement had expected on his return.

63

As the contradictions within Peronism became increasingly acute, so the violence escalated. Paramilitary groups and right wing death squads emerged and instances of torture and murder of militants grew. But it was following Perón's death in July 1974 that political terror against the left became an instrument of government. Perón was succeeded by his wife Isabel, who was closely associated with the semi-fascist wing of the movement represented by Lopez Rega who Isabel kept on as Minister of Social Welfare. Together with two notorious police torturers and members of the armed forces, Lopez Rega set up the Argentine Anti-Communist Alliance (AAA). Its aim was to eliminate known or suspected militants. During Isabel Perón's government there were 535 victims of para-military action, including workers, students, lawyers, doctors and teachers.

Initially the *Montoneros* gave Isabel their critical support, but in early September 1974 they went underground and declared all-out war on her government. The ERP, which had been declared illegal shortly before Perón's inauguration, stepped up its military activity. At the same time, the economic situation in Argentina was becoming critical. The impact of the international recession had become very serious in 1975 and inflation began to rise dramatically. The resignation of Perón's economy minister, José Gelbard, signalled the collapse of Perón's programme of national capitalist development. Those in power now favoured a shift towards orthodox right-wing economic policies including an attempt to curb the power of the trade union movement.

But the workers' movement was gradually accepting the necessity of confrontation with the Peronist government led by Isabel. A strike in the key steel producing area of Villa Constitución in early 1975 was a foretaste of the workers' renewed militancy. Union elections a few months earlier in the local metalworkers union had resulted in an overwhelming victory for those who opposed the old Peronist bureaucracy. The new leaders demanded a 70 per cent wage increase and workers control over industrial health. A month long struggle ensued in which four successive strike committees were arrested. Although the strike did not achieve its objectives, it marked an important turn in the movement.

In June 1975 a new economy minister, Celestino Rodrigo, was appointed, a member of the inner right-wing circle of the government. Rodrigo tried to push through a new austerity plan involving a new devaluation of the peso, increases in the prices of public goods and services, in some cases of more than 100 per cent, and a severe limitation on wage increases to under 40 per cent while inflation rose 102 per cent from June to August alone. The working class fought back and the last months of Isabel's government were marked by a struggle for power between the union base of the Peronist movement, whose bureaucratic leadership came under increasing pressure from the rank and file, and the right wing of the movement in government.

In July 1975 a massive wave of wildcat strikes spread throughout the country and the CGT was forced to call a 48-hour general strike. In Córdoba and Santa Fe provinces a new type of rank and file movement grew up formed by district coordinating bodies known as 'coordinadoras' of factory militants and workers commissions.

The Peronist movement was coming apart. By the end of 1975 the split between those who remained loyal to Isabel (known as *verticalistas*) and those who questioned her right to head the Peronist movement (known as *anti-verticalistas*) had deepened and was seriously dividing the trade union leadership. The 'moderate right' in the trade union bureaucracy together with similar minded politicians managed to secure the removal of both Lopez Rega and Rodrigo from the cabinet, aided by the rank and file pressure and the general turmoil in the countryu. A new Minister of Economy, Alberto Cafiero, who had links with the trade union leadership, took over in August 1975.

The economy was in a state of chaos. The industrial sector was in deep depression, unemployment had shot up from 2.3 per cent to 6 per cent in Greater Buenos Aires and to 7.5 per cent in Córdoba and other centres of the badly hit car industry. Industrial output fell in the third quarter of 1975 by 5.6 per cent. The external situation remained critical and inflation was reaching an alarming level, fuelled by the struggle over the distribution of income as workers tried to maintain their standard of living. In this crisis the Peronist government abandoned its traditional opposition to the IMF and began negotiations for 'compensatory funding' to relieve the balance of payments problems. However, the IMF rejected the economic plan put forward by the government as it did not include a drastic reduction in wages, it aimed at full employment and did not contain proposals for a sufficient reduction in public expenditure. The government sought the cooperation of the US State Department and eventually an agreement was reached, but the IMF's less than enthusiastic response made it difficult for the government to secure further external funding from the private banks.

As the crisis intensified, rumours of a military coup began to grow. The army had been deeply involved in the repression of the guerrilla movement. In 1975 it succeeded in defeating the rural guerrilla campaign launched by the ERP in Tucuman and had heavily infiltrated the *Montoneros*. It had also begun to form death squads and politicians, trade unionists, students and professionals suspected of involvement in the guerrilla movement began to disappear. But while the guerrilla struggle was used to justify the subsequent coup and indeed might have accelerated it, it was the increasing mobilizations of the working class which was the most serious concern of the armed forces and their allies within the Argentine economic elite.

The workers' mobilizations increased at the beginning of 1976 after Isabel had dismissed the moderate members of the government and a new Economy minister, Mondelli, was appointed to launch yet another austerity programme. Severe wage limits were decreed once again and there was a proposal to dismiss half a million public sector employees. Real wages fell 26 per cent between December 1975 and March 1976. A series of strikes, mostly a result of spontaneous working class action, shook the country. A section of the trade union leadership led by Victorio Calabró called a series of 24-hour and 48-hour strikes but then began to retreat and negotiate with some members of the armed forces. For the workers who still looked to Peronism for their political leadership this sort of betrayal was confusing and demoralizing. The Peronist left on the other hand was still engaged in the armed struggle rather than building on the mobilizations of the rank and file workers' movement. This was the situation in which Isabel Perón's government was overthrown by the military on 24 March 1976.

Economic Restructuring and Political Repression, 1976-1981

The military *coup* of March 1976 had the support of most Argentine industrialists, landowners and financiers, who had refused to accept the reformist project attempted by Perón. They sought a solution to the country's economic crisis which would squeeze workers' living standards rather than their own profits. No Peronist government could successfully implement such a strategy as it always had to take account of its trade union base. The *coup* was also welcomed by a sector of the middle class, alienated by the chaos and disorders of the previous years and who now saw a possibility of a restoration of law and order.

The military government headed by General Jorge Videla, aimed to transform Argentina's political system. In particular it aimed to weaken decisively the power of the organized working class and its Peronist political leadership. In this way they hoped to create the political conditions necessary for the restructuring of the economy. Such a restructuring was to involve the dismantling of all restrictions on the operation of a free market economy, in particular those engendered by state interventionism. The liberalization of the economy would end the protectionism behind which many inefficient industries were considered to have sheltered in the past. Argentina would be brought back into the international economy in those areas where its productive potential proved most competitive, and it had a comparative advantage. It was a strategy long advocated by landowners, bankers and those involved in the import-export business.

It was the political struggle over the distribution of income in Argentina, which in the eyes of the military had reduced the country to its present state of crisis. Henceforth, democratic political structures were to give way to the 'apoliticism' of technocrats. Political parties and political activities would be banned and the technocrats would be free to elaborate a coherent economic project for the country unhindered by the need to appease a political base. The man chosen for this purpose and appointed economy minister was José Martinez de Hoz, an old Etonian and Harvard graduate. He was hardly a 'pure' technocrat as he was a wealthy industrialist landowner and financier. But he was a monetarist whose close ties with the international financial centres were considered particularly important if Argentina was to renegotiate its large foreign debt and restore the confidence of foreign investors in the economy.

The military set about their political tasks with vigour. They launched what the new President referred to as the 'third world war' against 'communist subversion'. The methods used were commensurate with the most brutal of wars and it has since been renamed the 'dirty war'. Suspects were kidnapped, mostly by paramilitary forces connected with one branch or other of the armed forces, tortured and 'made to disappear'. In other words their deaths have never been admitted by the authorities, although many of them have undoubtedly been murdered. According to the Argentine human rights committees, an estimated 15,000 people disappeared in these years.

Officially the military's war was against the guerrilla movement, or 'terrorists' as they were called in an attempt to make their elimination more acceptable to international opinion. But the military's interpretation of a 'subversive' went far beyond those actually engaged in armed struggle. President Videla himself suggested this when he stated: 'A terrorist is not just someone with a gun or a bomb but also someone who spreads ideas that are contrary to Western and Christian civilization'. So the repression fell upon trade unionists, students, doctors, teachers, and political activists of all persuasions. The accompanying testimony gives an indication of the state terror employed by the junta in these years for which it was universally condemned by every international body concerned with human rights.

While the military was engaged in its war against subversion, Martinez de Hoz was attempting to restore order to the economy.

Testimony from the Argentine Concentration Camps

In this testimony, we denounce to the world the terrorism of the state, not only in our name, but also in memory of all those who were assassinated in the streets, on the torture tables, and those who met their end secretly in the 'transfer': the planned, massive assassination which was the real and tragic destination of most of the people who disappeared.

Club Atlético (in the Federal Capital) operated as a sort of prisoner depot where the only law was terror. It was an underground, unventilated place, without any natural light, and was very damp and very hot. The cells, called 'tubos' (pipes) were very small. Discipline was very strict and we were shackled, which prevented us from moving more than 40 centimetres and hurt our ankles. We had tight cloth blindfolds over our eyes. At first, we suffered from infections, since the cloth was dirty. The infection made our eyes swell, but after a time we became immune and the swelling did not recur. We could neither talk nor move and were always sitting or lying down; when two prisoners were together in one cell, they could not talk. If there was just one noise, all the section was punished. There were two sections. The guards wore soft footwear, and opened the doors suddenly to see if we were standing up or not wearing the blindfolds — for we were blindfolded even in the cells. If they saw us move our hands, even if it was not to touch the blindfold, they beat us until we lost consciousness.

As regards physical torture, we were all treated alike, the only differences being in intensity and duration. Naked, we were bound hand and foot with thick chains or straps to a metal table. Than an earthing cable was attached to one of our toes and the torture began.

For the first hour they would apply the 'picana' (cattle prod) to us, without asking any questions. The purpose of this was, as they put it, 'to soften you up, and so that we'll understand one another.' They went on like this for hours. They applied it to the head, armpits, sexual organs, anus, groin, mouth and all the sensitive parts of the body. From time to time they threw water over us or washed us, 'to cool your body down so that you'll be sensitive again.'

Between sessions of the 'picana', they would use the 'submarino', (holding our heads under water), hang us up by our feet, hit us on the sexual organs, beat us with chains, put salt on our wounds and use any other method that occurred to them. They would also apply 220-volt direct current to us and we know that sometimes — as in the case of Irma Necich — they used what they called the 'piripipi', a type of noise torture.

There was no limit to the torture. It could last for one, two, five or ten days. Everything was done under the supervision of a doctor, who checked our blood-pressure and reflexes: 'We're not going to let you die before time. We've got all the time in the world, and this will go on indefinitely.' That is exactly how it was, because when we were on the verge of death they would stop and let us be revived. The doctor injected serum and vitamins and when we had more or less recovered they began to torture us again.

Many of the prisoners could not endure this terrible treatment and fell into a coma. When this happened, they either left them to die or else 'took them off to the military hospital.' We never heard of any of these prisoners again.

Oscar Alfredo Gonzáles and Horácio Cid de la Paz, *Testimony on Secret Detention Camps in Argentina*, Amnesty International, London 1980.

Price controls were eliminated and wage controls introduced. The implementation of such measures was facilitated by the banning of strikes (strikers faced five to ten years in prison), and trade union activity (such as collective bargaining, the election of officers, and the holding of branch meetings). The CGT and its 36 main affiliated unions were put under the control of military administrators. Cuts in public spending were announced as well as a plan to sell off public sector companies. According to Martinez de Hoz's strategy, the export sector was to provide the dynamism necessary to stimulate the economy.

It was also considered essential to attract foreign investment (see Table 4, page 128). The legislative measures established by the Peronist government to control foreign investment were dismantled and court cases against Siemens, Shell, Exxon, First National Bank and other companies for violating these laws were dropped. All limits on the activities of foreign companies, including those on the repatriation of profits, were lifted. Martinez de Hoz himself was quoted in *La Nación* on 28 July 1976: 'The new law will give guarantees to the foreign investor which are unique in the world'. Nevertheless, despite this legislation, foreign capital did not flood into Argentina for the purposes of productive investment but rather as a speculative enterprise to take short term advantage of high interest rates.

Martinez de Hoz also began the process of lowering tariff barriers so that within five years protectionism would be reduced to a minimum. Only the most 'efficient' industries able to compete with the influx of cheap imported goods would be expected to survive. This was accompanied after 1977 by a policy of using the exchange rate and an overvalued peso as an anti-inflationary instrument. By maintaining the monthly devaluation rate below the level of inflation prices would be forced to decline. This policy gave further advantages to imported industrial goods which entered the country at prices well below those produced locally.

It was the smaller and medium-sized firms with little bargaining power which suffered most from this competition. The sectors of industry most affected were textiles. In *La Opinión*, 19 December 1978, the Federación de Industriales Textiles was quoted as saying: 'The textile industry is today threatened by the growing volume of imports, which . . . could come to substitute about 30 per cent of national textile production by the middle of next year'. Electronics machinery, tools, metallurgy, plastics and the print industry were all placed at risk. The largest firms in these sectors were transnational corporations, who by virtue of their company network, were able to convert part of their operations into intrafirm transactions.

The smaller firms suffered heavily not only from the lowering of tariff barriers but also from the high interest rates which the government maintained in order to defend the value of the peso. The larger firms on the other hand could resort to foreign borrowing. The high interest rates encouraged both domestic and foreign investors to speculate with short-term financial operations rather than to go into long-term capital investments. Thus while high levels of domestic savings and foreign reserves were maintained these disguised the ephemeral nature of the speculative investments involved.

Industry was also seriously affected by the collapse of the internal market. Although imported luxury goods continued to find a market in the high income sector, the fall in real wages by 50 per cent drastically reduced demand. Workers in the public sector were particularly badly hit. The fall in imports of capital goods during this period reflected the crisis in local industry. By April and May 1980 there was a wave of bankruptcies in Argentine industrial firms which dragged with them a number of major national banks although these had initially benefited from the government's interest rate policies.

It was soon apparent that the economy had failed to respond to Martinez de Hoz's formula. The healthiest sector of the economy for most of his period in office was the export sector, helped by purchases from the Soviet Union. But by 1979 the previously sound trade balance was deteriorating and by 1980 it was in deficit by US$2.4 billion. The inflation rate began to fall in 1980, but the fall was much less and later than theory had suggested it ought to be. Public expenditure continued to be extremely high. Indeed figures showed that Argentina combined almost the highest rates of growth in public consumption in the world with negative growth in private consumption, and very low growth in gross domestic investment. Martinez de Hoz had difficulties in dealing with this aspect of the Argentine economy since those responsible for the high level of public spending were primarily the military forces themselves, both through defence and security expenditure and through their involvement in a number of inefficient state enterprises. Tax evasion and corruption in Argentine public life had increased considerably in recent years and also contributed to the problems of the public sector.

Martinez de Hoz's policies did not go unchallenged. Despite the repression, the labour movement resisted the attack on its living standards and trade union rights. Strikes took place in the motor industry and amongst the power workers in 1976; rail, oil, bank and maritime workers in 1977; doctors and railway workers struck in 1978, and in April 1979 there was a general strike in which 30 per cent of the labour force participated. The repression during these strikes was harsh. The leaders often 'disappeared' during the disputes. In 1977 during the rail workers stoppage, a leader calling for strike action was shot dead on the spot.

In November 1979 the government published its new labour code, the Ley de Asociaciones Profesionales. It abolished national labour confederations including the CGT, banned trade unions from all political activity, outlawed the closed shop arrangement and gave the state the right to take over the social welfare provided by the unions. The movement's resistance to this legislative onslaught was weakened by its continued divisions. The Group of 20 *(Comisión de los 20)* generally represented the trade unions whose leadership was replaced by the military, while the Group of 25 *(Comisión de los 25)* is one of the successors to the CGT, grouping those unions not formally controlled by the military, and representing more radical Peronist tendencies. In October 1979, the CNT and the '25' agreed to form a central national labour body to negotiate with the regime on labour issues. This became known as the Conduccion Unica de los Trabajadores Argentinos (CUTA) and was tacitly recognized by the government. But in June 1980 CUTA split over the issue of representation in the International Labour Organization (ILO) and the International Confederation of Free Trade Unions (ICFTU).

Within the armed forces themselves there were substantial differences over economic policy, and only a small majority supported the strategy of Martinez de Hoz. A high level of state participation in the economy had developed in Argentina over the last fifty years irrespective of the changes in government. The armed forces themselves had become deeply involved in a number of public sector enterprises. As early as the 1920s a number of army officers had put forward the need to industrialize as a way of reducing Argentina's dependence on agricultural and livestock exports. In 1941 the Dirección General de Fabricaciones Militares (DGFM) run by the army, was set up, and this today represents the military's own

71

industrial complex. It runs 12 military plants and has a majority share-holding in at least seven other companies involved in the steel, timber, electronics, petrochemicals and construction industries and a significant share in a further ten companies. It employs an estimated 14,000 people directly and another 16,000 in its associated companies and has an annual turnover of US$1.2 billion. The armed forces are particularly concerned with the development of an independent technology and the rapid adaptation of foreign military technology acquired under licensing arrangements. In addition, retired army officers often sit on the boards of large and medium-sized Argentine firms. The navy and the air force also have their own supply industries.

There is thus a large section of the Argentine armed forces which believes that a strong national industry is important to the country on security grounds. This group has played an important role in the attempts by the private industrialists to resist the reduction in tariff barriers, particularly in industries which the military considers to be of strategic importance, such as steel and electronics. At times, links have been made with those associated with the *desarrollista* ideas of ex-President Arturo Frondizi, who also believed that national industry was essential to the country's development.

The navy has been particularly critical of Martinez de Hoz's policies. Retired Admiral Emilio Massera has been one of his most outspoken critics, undoubtedly as part of Massera's own bid for a political role in Argentina. Massera is known to have made links with right wing Peronists, and has tried to build up an image as a democrat. Typical of Massera's style was a speech in May 1978 in which he claimed that foreign investment had not yet begun to flow freely into Argentina because of the junta's political failure to create the necessary climate of confidence. He contrasted the 'imaginative statistics' produced by the Minister for the Economy with the reality of 'a people struggling desperately to survive and the serious worries of local industrialists'. Massera also advocated a tough stance on the Falklands/Malvinas conflict with Britain during 1976-77, and an occupation of the islands in the Beagle Channel dispute with Chile. Such nationalist initiatives, he believed, would serve to unite the nation as well as giving the navy some advantage over the army.

Inter-service rivalries (only the air force does not seem to have ambitions to the presidency) have beset the junta since its inception. These are further complicated by the divisions within each branch of the armed forces, for instance between the infantry and the cavalry in the army. Many of the divisions centre on the future role of the armed forces: how to ensure their control over any transition to civilian government, how to prevent investigation into the atrocities of the 'dirty war', and future relations between the armed forces and the civilian parties and politicians. Discussions began on these themes early on in the junta's life.

By May 1978 following a lengthy conclave, a formula was reached which confirmed the army's assertion of authority over the two other services. Videla was allowed to continue as president until March 1981, though he would retire as army commander on 1 August 1978. In September 1978, Videla announced that the first phase of the military government had been completed, and that it was time to formulate a plan for the country's future. The three services submitted separate draft plans, and a commission was set up to produce a single plan from this. But no coherent plan emerged from these discussions, reflecting the strength of the divisions which still persisted.

General Roberto Viola, Videla's successor as Commander-in-Chief of the army from 1978 to 1979 and a man closely associated with the President, took over office from him on 29 March 1981. Martinez de Hoz had previously announced that he would retire at the same time. The fact than an orderly succession had taken place impressed many observers. Viola was associated, as was Videla, with the more conciliatory line within the armed forces and there were hopes that Viola might initiate the long-awaited dialogue with the civilian political forces. But Viola took over the presidency as Argentina went through its worst financial crisis since 1976.

Viola to Galtieri

Viola's task was formidable. The 1980 treasury deficit was double that of 1979 and the total public sector deficit was running at 4 per cent of GDP. The trade balance had moved into the red. The country's foreign debt, which had stood at US$19 billion at the beginning of 1980 had rocketed to US$30 billion by the end of the year. The international financial community continued to lend to Argentina as it was considered a country with a sound long-term future with considerable potential as an exporter of manufactured goods, food and energy. Indeed the volume of Argentine exports had increased father than any other country in Latin America except Mexico. But sustained economic growth proved an elusive goal. Average annual growth rates for the period 1976 to 1980 were down to 1.6 per cent, compared with 4.4 per cent in 1961-70, and 2.8 per cent in 1971-75.

The new economics team under Finance Minister Lorenzo Sigaut, was committed to a modification in the strategy adopted by Martinez de Hoz. He began by devaluing the peso, and providing some assistance to industry in credit and taxes. But he failed to inspire confidence. All the indicators pointed to a deepening of the recession. In June 1981 the country was shaked by its third serious financial crisis in three months, involving a major panic on the foreign exchange markets. Foreign reserves fell by US$308 million in one day.

The growing rate of bankruptcies and sackings in manufacturing industry, a sector which accounted for 30 per cent of total employment and 37 per cent of GDP, reflected the fact that it was on the point of collapse. The extremely high interest rates and level of indebtedness threatened the survival of many companies. An estimated 100,000 jobs had been lost in the steel industry since 1976; in the textile industry on the outskirts of Buenos Aires, the 180 companies which had employed 9,000 people in 1978 were now reduced to 120 companies employing only 3,200 workers. Most car plants had been laying off people for months. Even Ford, which had done very well in Argentina in 1979 and 1980 assisted by the demise of its competitors (General Motors and Citroën had withdrawn from Argentina, Chrysler had sold out to Volkswagen, and Fiat had merged with Peugeot) was now deep in trouble. In fact Juan Maria Courard, president of the Ford Motor Company of Argentina was making public statements critical of the government. At a press conference to launch a new line of trucks in September 1981 he stated:

For months now we've been waiting to see what the govenment will do. Always waiting. The high interest rates, the most worrying factor, have been discussed at all levels within the government, but still nothing has been done to stop them climbing. No industrialist in the world can work with interest rates in excess of 11 per cent a month.

Import competition and the rapid fall in demand during 1981 were also held responsible for the industry's problems.

The new govenment's failure to bring about an economic recovery further enhanced divisions within the army and the opposition to Viola's presidency. Viola's position in the armed forces had been weakened in the 1980 promotions and retirements. Differences were becoming increasingly marked between Viola and the three man junta. While Videla had been able to count on the support of his army commander, Robert Viola himself, the new commander, General Leopoldo Galtieri, did not support the president. In this situation Viola made a bid to reach an understanding with civilian politicians. Contacts between the political parties and the presidency reached their most active since the 1976 coup. The release of Isabel Perón, despite much opposition within the armed forces, helped pave the way for discussions with the Peronists. A five-party political front called the Multipartidaria, had emerged made up of the Radicals, Peronists, the *desarrollistas* in ex-President Frondizi's party the MID, the

Would You Buy A New Car From This Company?

The Ford Motor Company took a full-page advertisement in the Argentine national press at the beginning of 1977 to send the junta the following New Year greeting:

<table>
<tr>
<td>

1976
Argentina
Gets Back on the Right Track

1977
New Year of Faith and Hope
For All Argentines of Good
Will

Ford Motor Company and its
Staff Pledge their Participation
in the Efforts to Fulfill The
Nation's Great Destiny

Again Ford Give You More

Ford Motor Argentina S.A.
y su red de Concesionarios.

</td>
<td>

1976
Nuevamente la Argentina
encuentra su camino.

1977
Nuevo año de fé y esperanza
para todos los argentinos
de buena voluntad.

Ford Motor Argentina y su gente
comprometen su participación
en el esfuerzo para la realización
de los grandes destinos de la Patria.

Nuevamente Ford le da más.

Ford Motor Argentina S.A.
y su red de Concesionarios.

</td>
</tr>
</table>

The year Argentina got 'back on the right track' was also the year in which General Videla took power unconstitutionally to forestall elections and oversee the killing of more than 2,000 people, the imprisonment and abduction of many thousands more.

An Earlier Advertisement
In that same year, in September, the government published Decree 21,400, the so-called Law of Industrial Security. This banned any action by workers that might lead to strikes, interruption or reduction of work levels or standards which could in any way prejudice production. Article 5 provides for sentences of from one to six years in jail for offenders — 'unless the act in question should constitute a more serious crime.' The same punishment faces those accused of incitement to strike, while *public* incitement carries a sentence of from three to ten years.

On 9 September, a week after the Decree came into force, Ford was also advertising in the main newspapers, though this time they could hardly pretend to be speaking on behalf of their employees: the advertisements were a warning to Ford workers to heed the effects of the decree . . . or face the consequences. For added emphasis the company next day sacked 98 workers at its main plant.

Committee for Human Rights in Argentina.

Intransigentes (a split from the Radicals) and the Christian Democrats. There were rumours in July 1981 that a deal had been struck between the parties and the president, that they would tone down their opposition to the government in return for allowing them some say in the choice of president in 1984 though this would not necessarily be through elections.

However, not all the opposition forces agreed with this line. On the left of the movement, a new grouping, the Peronistas Intransigentes, condemned any form of 'Peronism diluted by short-term alliances' or the search for an electoral solution without the prior establishment of democracy within the party. Although some political activity was now permitted, internal party elections were still prohibited so that no party could test the strength of the different factions emerging within it.

Within Peronism, politicians and trade union leaders had taken very different positions on the issue of 'dialogue' with the military. The official, traditional Peronist group is led by Deolindo Bittel with the support of a wide cross-section of the Peronist movement. They were willing to negotiate with the government. A smaller group centred on conservative provincial political bosses, led by Dr Matera, had come to support Emilio Massera's bid for power. A third section is led by Lorenzo Miguel and other leaders of the '62 organizations' which had opposed the political line of the CNT and rejected the 'dialogue'. A fourth group led by a lawyer Vicente Saadi, was outwardly hostile to negotiations, but kept the communication lines open.

The armed forces continued to be deeply divided in their attitude towards a return to civilian rule. Many feared that the renewed political activity might slip out of their control.

The fragmentation within the armed forces grew further as the economic crisis deepened. The hardliners were led by General Cristino Nicolaides, the commander of the powerful third army corps based in Córdoba. He maintained that subverion was still in operation in Argentina. In April 1980 he had stated: 'subversion, militarily defeated, has changed its strategy and tactics, and today has its centre of gravity in ideological penetration. Subversion is entrenched, and is waiting to pounce in every sector of national life.' General Galtieri was increasingly opposed to the president's liberalization programme. Galtieri's opposition reflected some of the resentment by cavalry officers against the infantry, represented by Viola and Videla, who had dominated the political process since the *coup*. Galtieri belived that a quick return to civilian rule could not be permitted. He had an eye to the past experience of military rule and made specific reference to this in a speech in July 1981:

In the last 50 years other military *procesos* faced with the proliferation of criticism, took the wrong path as though elections were the solution to the political problem. The history of those successive failures, the after-effects of which we are still suffering, leave us with the hard but wise lesson that we must not make the same mistake.

For its part, the navy was apparently moving towards the view that some staged return to constitutional rule should be planned.

It was becoming increasingly apparent that Viola was doomed. In the end of year promotions, Viola's supporters suffered a clear loss of influence. The majority of the generals loyal to Videla and Viola were retired, and new men mostly from the cavalry were in the ascendency, foremost among them being General Galtieri himself. In December 1981, after some painful negotiations in which the evident disunity within the armed forces could not be disguised, Viola was removed using his recent illness as the excuse and Galtieri appointed his successor. At the same time the armed forces seem to have concluded that it was time to return to March 1976 and the original objectives which inspired the *coup*. The appointment of Roberto Alemann to run the economy suggested a return to the era of Martinez de Hoz.

Galtieri and the Invasion

The internal coup which brough Galtieri to the presidency reflected the depth of the country's political crisis. The military's project for Argentina — the Process of National Reorganization *(Proceso de Reorganización Nacional)* as it was known — was in danger of total collapse. In the first years of the military govenment, the armed forces could unite around the repression of the guerrilla movement and all forms of 'subversion'. All branches of the armed forces had been deeply involved in the 'dirty-war' of 1976-79. But they could not agree on a more permanent political formula for the country's future. Official speeches referred to vague notions of establishing a 'stable, republican and federal democracy' through the establishment of a 'movement of national option'. But they were never translated into a firm project.

Apart from the divisions within the armed forces which undermined the elaboration of such a project, the military were unable to win any popular support for their continuation in office. Neither the main political force, Peronism, nor the second force, the Radical Party, would accept such a prospect, and they continued to seek a return to elections. But Viola's gradual liberalzation never became a reality.

Nor would the issue of the 'disappeared' persons go away. Middle class as well as working class families had lost sons and daughters,

Diabolical Angel

The Argentine surrender of South Georgia was signed by Captain Alfredo Astiz who had commanded the Argentine garrison on the island.

Astiz, aged 29, nicknamed the Blond Angel, formerly headed the GT33/2 kidnap squad based at the notorious *Escuela de Mecánica de la Armada*, the naval engineering college in Buenos Aires used as a torture camp. The squad was responsible for the kidnapping, torture and 'disappearance' of several hundred people.

In 1979 the squad was disbanded, and a number of officers given diplomatic posts. Some were based at Argentina's naval commission in London, from where numerous arms purchases were conducted. Their roles as torturers were exposed by a number of former victims in the ITV World in Action programme entitled 'The Men from Argentina', broadcast on 30 March 1981. Three women testified that these same men had been involved in torture and executions in the Escuela. Pregnant women were allowed to give birth, then killed, and their babies adopted by childless couples in the armed forces.

The same women identified the role of Astiz to the press. Ana Maria Marti's two children were kidnapped while she was being held, and Astiz forced them to watch her being tortured. 'Astiz was in charge of kidnapping operations', she claimed, 'He was so young, so innocent in appearance, it was difficult to believe he could be so cruel.'

Susana Burgos witnessed the shooting by Astiz of a young Swedish girl, Dagmar Hagelin, aged 17, on 26 January 1977, and saw her the following day inside the Escuela, handcuffed and paralysed by the bullet. She has never been seen since.

Astiz also infiltrated a group of relatives of 'disappeared' persons, posing as a human rights activist. He used this cover to arrange the kidnapping of two French nuns who were assisting the relatives. Sisters Alice Domon and Leonie Duquet were tortured in the Escuela, and it is believed that their bodies were dumped in the Parana river estuary.

Astiz was subsequently sent to Paris, and then Pretoria, as a naval attaché. Whilst in South Africa, a Durban newspaper, the *Sunday Tribune*, ran a series of articles in December 1981 exposing his past as a torturer. Although embarrassed by these revelations, Pretoria felt it would be unwise to deport Astiz immediately and risk alienating the Argentine junta, whose friendship was being cultivated.

Instead, Astiz was sent to a naval college in Muizenburg, near the Silvermine Maritime Command in the Cape Peninsula, where he underwent commando training, and was awarded a medal on completion of the course. This was only revealed during the Falklands war when the full extent of South Africa's naval assistance to Argentina was uncovered.

On his surrender to the British forces on South Georgia, Astiz was first imprisoned on Ascension Island, and later transferred to England, where he was housed in 'pleasant' conditions. All requests on the part of Sweden and France to question him were resisted, as Britain claimed that under the Geneva Convention, prisoners of war were not liable to answer for crimes committed in Argentina prior to the hostilities. Astiz was returned to Argentina unpunished, in the hope that three British journalists held in Ushuaia on 'espionage' charges would be released in an informal exchange.

In the July 1982 issue of the International Commission of Jurists' *ICJ Review*, published by this Geneva-based independent body of international lawyers, it was claimed that under present international law Britain had no option but to free Astiz. Modifications to the Geneva Convention enabling the holding of trials for crimes committed in other countries were recommended. It seems ludicrous that no mechanism was employed to bring Astiz, a known torturer, to trial. When it flies in the face of natural justice, as in this instance, international law stands discredited.

In due course the Argentine opposition hopes to try Astiz in his own country. Meanwhile the Blond Angel remains at large.

wives and husbands in the 'dirty war'. They were not disposed to forget their individual tragedies.

The failure of the economic policy had also served to isolate the military. Although the working class were more badly hit by the policies, the middle class had also seen its standard of living fall while many industrialists had gone bankrupt. Even the church, the most conservative in Latin America, had begun to criticize the government openly. In July 1981 the church published a document which undermined the military's justification of the 'dirty war'. In it the bishops stated: 'We must distinguish between the justification for the war against the guerrillas, and the methods used in this war.' On 7 November 1981 the church gave tacit backing to a demonstration led by the Peronist CGT 'for peace, bread and work'. It gathered 15,000 people and was the largest deomonstration since the military had taken power in 1976.

Galtieri was aware that in order to survive politically he had to introduce some major initiatives both on the economic and the political front.

Economically Argentina was still in a deep recession. GDP had fallen a record 11.4 per cent in the third quarter of 1981, industrial production had declined by 22.9 per cent, and real wages fell by 19.2 per cent. Alemann's policies signalled a return to reliance on the free market and foreign investment. He described his aims as to 'deflate, deregulate and denationalize'.

He devalued the peso, announced measures to cut the enormous public sector deficit and to sell off public companies to the private sector and introduced an indefinite wage freeze. 'The economy will recover through exports and investment, and not, at least in the short term, through domestic consumption', he announced in January 1982.

Politically, Galtieri tired to combine his programme of economic austerity with an attempt to make a populist appeal. He had come to accept that some measure of liberalization would have to be introduced in the medium term and he announced plans to bring in a statute which would outline the permitted limits for party political activity. But Galtieri hoped at the same time to build his own base, which would ensure a place for himself and the armed forces in the country's political future once the transition to constitutional rule had begun. He was expected to retire from the post of commander of the army in December 1981, and in order to continue in government beyond 1984, he also had to consolidate his support within the army.

One of the first indications of Galtieri's plans to appeal to the people came early in his presidency when he made a public statement of his assets to show that he was not going to use his office for personal enrichment. He admitted to possessing wordly goods worth US$180,000 and promised to return his presidential salary to the treasury. Subsequently he began to make 'informal' public appearances, shaking hands with the elderly and kissing babies. In February 1982 a free barbecue was organized in Victorica, a small provincial town. 13,000 people were given free transport to attend the event and Galtieri spoke of the need to form 'a political force which will represent in organic fashion, an independent current of national opinion which until now has remained diffuse'.

But it is in the field of foreign policy that Galtieri began to play out his political ambitions most vigorously. Throughout 1981, there were indications that Argentina was going to take a hard line on a number of foreign policy issues. Galtieri himself as army commander played an important role in these moves.

One of the most important long-standing disputes was that with Chile over the three islands in the Beagle Channel. This had brought the country to the brink of war in 1979. On 29 April 1981 the Argentine govenment closed its border with Chile in response to what it claimed was Chilean 'provocation' — the arrest of two Argentine officers in Chile on charges of espionage. Galtieri himself then personally ordered the mobilization of troops from the third army corps and the eighth mountain infantry brigade. To most observers this was a deliberate over-reaction as a number of Chilean army officers were in Argentine jails on similar charges. But Argentina was anxious to modify any proposal likely to come out of the Vatican mediation of the dispute by asserting its strength early on. With Galtieri in the presidency, the crisis flared up again. His right-wing Foreign Minister Nicanor Costa Mendez made the dispute one of his top priorities. On 21 January 1982 the government repudiated the 1972 treaty with Chile which provided for arbitration of frontier disputes through the International Court of Justice.

During 1981 the army began to shift its foreign policy into close alignment with that of the United States and the 'Western and Christian world'. This was facilitated by Reagan's assumption of the presidency, and his wish to restore good relations with the junta. Relations with his predecessor, Jimmy Carter, had become very strained as a result of Carter's insistence on raising human rights issues as a factor in relations between the two countries. In September 1981 General Vernon Walters, former US Secretary of State Alexander Haig's special adviser on Latin America, visited Buenos Aires. He is reported to have requested the Argentine govenment not to build up tension with Chile, to revise the country's trade agreement with the Soviet Union and to modify its support for the 1980 coup in Bolivia. The United States wished to purge the Bolivian government of officers most directly involved in the international drug trade and did not want Argentine interference in such action. The US also requested the deployment of Argentine troops in Sinai as part of a peacekeeping force sponsored by Egypt and the United States and asked the Argentine government to step up its aid to the Salvadorean junta and to be ready to send troops to Central America as part of an inter-American force. Walters also made it clear that his government wished to restore military aid to the country but it insisted efforts should be made to return to more democratic forms of government.

Galtieri in particular seems to have been responsive to American requests. He himself had gone to the United States in September 1981 at the invitation of the US army chief of staff.

In November 1981 Galtieri paid another visit to Washington for the gathering of American army leaders and further cemented the relationship with the US. Defence Secretary Caspar Weinberger described him as a 'magnificent person' and National Security adviser Richard Allen called him an 'impressive general'. As President Galtieri continued to offer the US substantial support for its policies in Central America, an estimated 200 advisers were sent to the region and there were indications that further support would be forthcoming if requested. Some newspapers began to describe Galtieri's presidency as an 'open and militant alliance with the US'. It is likely that Galtieri assumed that its ally would not oppose an attempt to recover the

Malvinas. Haig's off the record remark about the islands after the invasion 'they have been a pimple on the ass of progress for 200 years, and I guess someone just decided to lance it' suggests that it was initially the Secretary of State's attitude.

There were a number of indications in the first three months of 1982 that the government was planning to occupy the islands. A report in *La Prensa* on 29 January from a columnist with close links with the armed forces stated that Argentina was preparing to present Britain with a virtual ultimatum for settling their dispute over the Malvinas and that the possibility of military action was not excluded. The navy was particularly in favour of such action. There was a belief that an occupation would be relatively easy, and that the British government would be unlikely to react strongly to such action.

In February 1982, Galtieri was reported to have secured a commitment to neutrality in a meeting with the Uruguayan president should Argentina take military action on the Malvinas.

In March 1982, the Argentine secretary-general of the Organization of American States (OAS), Alejandro Orfila, announced that 'soon the Argentine flag would be waving again in the Islas Malvinas'. The same month, an Argentine air force Hercules C-130 aircraft landed on the Malvinas.

The occupation finally took place on 2 April 1982. There can be no doubt that the action was linked to the country's profound internal political and economic crisis. The Malvinas issue was still a live grievance in the minds of most Argentinians and the occupation was guaranteed to be immensely popular. Galtieri himself had much to gain from such action. Two days before the invasion 10,000 people had demonstrated against the government, over 1,000 people were arrested and at least one person killed, a miner from Mendoza named Ortiz. On 6 April, shortly after the invasion an estimated quarter of a million people flocked the streets of Buenos Aires in support of the occupation. But there was a danger sign for the President and his colleagues in that the slogans shouted showed that the population made a sharp distinction between support for the occupation and support for the military government.

Britain and the Argentine Junta

The 1976 *coup* was undoubtedly welcomed by the international financial community. A sign of this was the readiness with which the IMF moved to ease the new government's financial burden. In September 1976 it granted a loan of US$290 million. Martinez de Hoz's economic policy closely fitted the views of the IMF on how to run a healthy economy. Thus it showed the Argentine government great favour. This IMF seal of approval enabled Argentina to negotiate loans with private banks. British banks figured quite prominently. Lloyds Bank International· headed a consortium of banks which loaned up to US$75 million to Argentina in July 1976. Later that same month, Martinez de Hoz visited Britain in search of loans and told *The Times* on 28 July that he had received from Great Britain, West Germany, France and the United States loans larger than anything the country had known in the past few years. The most important banks sustaining the Argentine external debt of an estimated US$34 billion by the end of 1981 were: from the United States, the Manufactures Hanover Corporation, the Morgan Guaranty Trust and Chase Manhattan; from France, the Credit Lyonnais; from Germany, the Deutsche Bank; and in Britain, Lloyds. An estimated US$2 billion were owed to British banks at the time of the Falklands/Malvinas crisis. London is also the headquarters of the Euro-dollar market through which many loans to Argentina were negotiated.

Apart from its involvement in loans, British investments to Argentina represented only 0.8 per cent of total foreign investment in Argentina. Britain's share of Argentine trade is only 3 per cent (see Table 6, page 129). In 1980 Argentine imports from Britain were worth about US$344 million against exports of US$226 million.

Although the British involvement in the Argentine economy is not great the Conservative government clearly saw Argentina as offering good possibilities for increasing business. The human rights record of the junta was never taken into account in any of the commercial and financial dealings. It was generally assumed that the restoration of law and order with the military *coup* was a positive advance over the chaos of previous years and the excesses in terms of human rights violations were merely 'unfortunate'. Michael Frenchard wrote in *The Times'* 1977 special report on Banking and Finance in Latin America:

Attempts to spread Cubanism to the Latin American mainland have been largely balked by the individual countries, particularly those in the southern half of the continent, which have established a so far unofficial alliance, the 'Southern Cone Pact' to combat the growth of communism in the region. Unfortunately in many cases military regimes have overreacted in their drive against attempted communist inspired takeovers. Bearing in mind the characteristic temperament of the Latin this should not have been entirely unexpected, but, in the case of Chile and Argentina it has led to a much tarnished image abroad, often deliberately so, in a number of instances. This has resulted in a mute misunderstanding . . .

British exports to Argentina doubled between 1976 and 1978. In that year Lord Nelson, Chairman of GEC, headed a group of 20 British businessmen on a visit to Argentina. In July 1979 the Conservative government restored diplomatic relations with Argentina at ambassadorial level. In June of the following year Martinez de Hoz met with Prime Minister Thatcher, Lord Carrington, Geoffrey Howe and Peter Walker and called for Britain 'to hurry up and be partners in our economic development'. Nicolas Ridley, Minister of State at the Foreign Office, stated that Britain and Argentina have 'good relations' a notably more positive description than the 'regular contact' used to describe relations with Brazil, Chile and Paraguay.

In May 1980 Cecil Parkinson, then Minister of Trade, when asked in parliament if he intended to increase trade with Argentina, replied: 'I believe civil trade with other countries should be determined by commercial considerations and not by the character of the governments concerned. It is my objective to increase our trade worldwide'. In August he led a trade delegation to Argentina. Trade relations were stepped up in 1981.

In June the Midland Bank led a group of industrialists on a trade mission to Argentina, seeking to expand the Argentine export market. After meetings with trade associations, Malcolm Wilcox, chief general manager of Midland, reported that 'real business has already resulted'. In September the Export Credit Guarantee Department guaranteed a loan of US$10 million to enable UK supplies of capital goods and associated services to obtain financing for exports to Argentina. That same month Agriculture Minister Peter Walker returned from a 10-day mission to Argentina and Brazil and declared: 'We could double or treble our trade' with Argentina and Brazil. The enthusiasm of the British government to foster trade with Latin America contrasted sharply with its silence on the issue of human rights. Even when the British government had a chance to give concrete assistance to victims of the repression in Argentina by expanding its refugee programme, it failed to respond.

After the Chilean *coup* in 1973, and again in 1976 after the military takeover in Argentina, pressure was put on the Labour government of the day to assist Latin American political refugees. The response was not encouraging. Long bureaucratic delays and the need for the refugees to be 'personally acceptable' (a criterion applied with the help of the CIA) hindered progress. By July 1974, only 87 Chilean refugees had been received by Britain, compared with 806 by Sweden, and 747 by West Germany. In June 1976, the United Nations High Commission for Refugees (UNHCR) appealed for international action to save the lives of Latin American refugees in Argentina. Britain responded by offering to accept 75 urgent cases. By February

1977, only 13 refugees from Argentina had arrived in Britain. The government was criticised in an editorial in *The Times* for failing to implement even its own very modest refugee programme.

It is clear that many Labour politicians were concerned that taking a stand on human rights issues would hinder the development of trading links with Argentina. A letter from Edmund Dell, then Secretary of State at the Department of Trade to the Foreign Secretary, David Owen, illustrates the point:

. . . several speakers expressed concern about the effect which our stand on human rights was having, and would continue to have for some time on our trade interests there. Since then, George (Lord) Nelson of GEC has written to Fred Catherwood, who as you know is Chairman of the British Overseas Trade Board, following up their discussion at the dinner. Apart from re-iterating his concern over our long term trade interests generally, he has particularly drawn attention to GEC's and British Aerospace's interest in selling the Hawk aircraft to Argentina (worth about £100 million). He belives that our decision not to receive Admiral Massera when he was in London during the summer weighed heavily with the Argentinians in deciding against buying British frigates. This contract would have been worth about £700 millon, more than five years' worth of exports at the present level and would obviously have been of major importance to UK shipbuilders.

I understand that you are at present considering whether or not General Agosti, Argentine Chief of Air Staff, should be invited here and be received at the appropriate level. Nelson and Catherwood both urge that we should invite him (I gather Agosti would like to come here), as failure to do so could damage our chances of success.

Together with West Germany, the United States, Israel and France, Britain has not hesitated to supply sophisticated weapons systems and support for Argentina's growing domestic arms industry (see Tables 8, 9 and 10, pp.131-3). The rapid growth of the Argentine armed forces makes them the second strongest in Latin America after Brazil. It is reported that as much as 35 per cent of national spending is directed to military purposes and that the domestic arms industry now employs 41,000 people.

Britain has been a traditional supplier of naval equipment (see tables). Type 42 destroyers, Seacat missile systems, Lynx naval helicopters, military electronics and communications systems, Canberra bombers and small arms all contributed to making Britain Argentina's fourth largest arms supplier. And with the arms sales went military training, exchange visists, secondments and the loaning of British military experts to Argentina. Whichever side might win the war in the South Atlantic, British arms manufacturers could not lose. As a Rolls Royce representative said of Argentina nine days after its armed forces had seized the Falkland Islands: 'As far as we are concerned, they are still our customers'.

Chronology of the Crisis

All information derived from British sources.

Date	Negotiations/ Mediation	Military Operations	Internal Reaction		International Reaction
			Britain	Argentina	
March 1982	Negotiations between Britain and Argentina end in an atmosphere of great tension.			Opposition to the government gains strength, with workers' strikes and demonstrations attacked by police.	
22-3				A group of Argentinian scrap metal merchants land in South Georgia and raise the Argentine flag.	
23-3/ 30-3	Tension increases. Negotiations continue.	British Navy despatches five ships.			
April 1-4	Deadlock over the crisis.				US offers mediation.
2-4	Break in diplomatic relations.	Argentina occupies the Falklands and dependencies. Clashes between British and Argentine troops. British marines surrender.			

All information derived from British sources.

Date	Negotiations/ Mediation	Military Operations	Internal Reaction		International Reaction
			Britain	Argentina	
3-4	UN Security Council passes resolution 502 for withdrawal of troops and peaceful settlement of the dispute.	British governor of the Falklands and certain other officials expelled.			Divided opinions on resolution 502. Some Latin American countries back Argentina.
5-4		Britain sends naval Task Force.	Lord Carrington resigns. Labour Party backs sending of Task Force.	Foreign minister Costa Mendez asks OAS countries to support Argentine action.	
6-4			Britain bans all Argentine imports.		Australia, New Zealand and Canada recall ambassadors from Buenos Aires.
7-4	Britain announces a 200-mile blockade around the islands.			Gen. Menendez installed as governor of islands.	Soviet Union worried about grain supplies from Argentina. European countries ban arm supplies to Argentina. Gibraltar talks with Spain postponed.
10-4					EEC countries ban imports from Argentina.

Date					
12-4	Mr Haig starts a series of trips between Argentina and Britain to reach peaceful agreement.				
13-4				Three British journalists arrested in Argentina charged with espionage.	
19-4	Haig continues his efforts to mediate.	Mr Pym goes to US.		Argentina invokes Rio Treaty to get military assistance from OAS member states.	
22-4		Task Force reaches the area.	Britain calls for US support if negotiations break down.	Galtieri visits islands. Parana, Argentina's largest private financial company, declared bankrupt. Argentina withdraws millions of US$ from the US.	
24-4	Sovereignty remains the main problem. Argentina agrees to the withdrawal of troops but wants to maintain flag and police force in Falklands.	The sea blockade is reinforced with a no-go air zone. A flotilla detached from main Task Force goes to South Georgia.	Shadow Foreign Secretary Healey meets Haig and says that if mediation fails, the US must abandon its neutrality and let UN take over the problem.	Government announces controls on 'enemy subjects' resident in the country.	Mexican President Lopez Portillo offers mediation should Haig mission fail.

All information derived from British sources.

Date	Negotiations/ Mediation	Military Operations	Internal Reaction		Argentina	International Reaction
			Britain		Argentina	
25-4	Haig offers to 'redouble' efforts for peace while saying that Rio Treaty wouldn't be appropriate or effective against UK.	British troops land and recover South Georgia. Argentine submarine damaged.	Polls show majority support for Thatcher in the conflict.		Demonstration supporting recovery of the Malvinas. Slogan 'Malvinas yes, government no' is used. Political parties call for government of national emergency.	Venezuela announces it will help Argentina if Galtieri asks. Virtually all Latin American states support Argentina.
27-4	Argentina rejects another visit by Haig.	Foot: 'explore every avenue in the search for a settlement'. David Owen: 'give a few more days to Haig'. Tony Benn: 'public opinion favours a more serious attempt at negotiations through UN'. Steel: 'are we willing to inflict heavy loss of life on both sides over a piece of territory whose title our government was prepared to give to Argentina 18 months ago?'	Foreign reserves fall by £190 million.			OAS meets and calls for ceasefire and negotiations. Venezuela excludes British banks from loan meeting in Caracas.

90

Date				
28-4		Labour Party's National Executive Committee unanimously backs party leader in calling on the government to appeal to the UN for help to solve crisis.	CGT warns government about economic consequences of conflict. The workers' union organizes demonstrations to support recovery of islands but against armed forces.	Soviet Union steps up its criticisms of 'Britain's adventurous escalation' of the conflict. Reports that Venezuela is posting troops in the border with Guyana. Israel refuses to introduce a formal embargo on arms sales to Argentina.
29-4	Argentina declares its own Malvinas exclusion zone.	Thatcher: 'If Argentina will not accept a negotiated solution, then reluctantly and with the greatest possible restraint we must use force'.		
30-4	Haig tells Britain that Argentina has rejected his proposals.	Pym: 'British people are deeply grateful to US and especially to Mr Haig for his remarkable efforts'.	Argentine government draws up an emergency economic package and press controls.	
May 1-5	Vulcan bomber and Sea Harrier attack Stanley Airport and Goose Green. Navy bombards Port	Labour splits over conflict. SDP-Liberal Alliance gives full backing to the government.		

All information derived from British sources.

Date	Negotiations/ Mediation	Military Operations	Internal Reaction		International Reaction
			Britain	Argentina	
1-5 contd.		Stanley. Argentine Mirage and Canberra attack British fleet (1 Mirage and 2 Canberra shot down). One British ship sustains superficial splinter damage.			
2-5	Pym has his first meeting with UN Secretary-General Perez de Cuellar.	*General Belgrano* Argentina's cruiser hit by torpedoes fired by British nuclear submarine outside exclusion zone.	The Ad Hoc Committee for Peace in the Falklands is set up to demonstrate every Sunday until the conflict finishes.		
3-5		Two armed Argentine patrol crafts hit British Sea King helicopter. Two RN Lynx helicopters engage Argentine ships; one sunk.			
4-5		*HMS Sheffield* is sunk by Argentine missile; 20 die. Sea Harrier shot down while attacking Port Stanley.			France, Holland and Italy express extreme anxiety about escalation of conflict. Soviet Union blames US for

6-5	Peruvian government initiates contacts to promote a cease-fire. This proves unsuccesful.	Britain increases the size of the Task Force. Two British Harrier jets are lost and pilots presumed killed.		crisis by putting pressure on Argentina while supporting Britain militarily. Juan Carlos of Spain offers to mediate. Ireland seeks removal of EEC sanctions on Argentina.
9-5	Perez de Cuellar begins formal talks on a ceasefire and long-term settlement.	Argentine Puma helicopter shot down.	Local elections in England and Wales. Conservative Party unexpectedly retains most of the seats, allegedly due to the 'Falklands factor'.	Venezuela reported to be withdrawing substantial sums from UK banks.
7-5		Exclusion zone extended to 12 miles off Argentine mainland.		French poll indicates majority of people refuse to support Britain if threat of major inolvement. Bonn expresses fear over escalation. Leaders of Belize, Colombia, Costa Rica, Honduras and Venezuela urge an end to hostilities.

All information derived from British sources.

Date	Negotiations/ Mediation	Military Operations	Internal Reaction		International Reaction
			Britain	**Argentina**	
10-5		Britain declares a 'controlled airspace' of 100 miles radius around Ascension Island.			
11-5		Argentine supply ship is hit by British aircraft in Falkland Sound (between East and West Falklands).	Mrs Thatcher and several government MPs are disappointed by the media coverage of the conflict. Opposition puts pressure on government to discuss diplomatic options available. Some disagreement between defence chiefs.		President Figueiredo of Brazil arrives in Washington but reduces his visit to one day, suspending attendance of receptions, concerts and exhibitions. At the IMF, leaders of developing countries express concern about economic measures taken against Argentina and recommend they be lifted.
12-5		Two Argentine aircraft shot down. Britain continues reinforcing Task Force. *Queen Elizabeth 2* sails to South Atlantic.	Some Conservative MPs urge the bombing of Argentine mainland.	Controversy within armed forces over possible Soviet economic and military aid. Five British and American journalists kidnapped and then released in	

Date					
13-5			Nott reasserts British right to use military options on Falklands.	Argentine industrial union criticizes Galtieri's monetarism. Argentina shows irritation at the holding of Captain Astiz.	Sweden and France accuse Astiz of being in charge of a concentration camp.
14-5		British marines raid Argentine military base on Pebble Island. 11 Argentine aircraft destroyed.			
16-5		Heavy bombardment of Argentine military installations in Falklands.		Galtieri says he is ready to see 4,000 or 40,000 Argeninians die in defence of their cause.	Italy and Ireland refuse to continue sanctions against Argentina.
19-5	British negative response to Argentine proposals.				
20-5	Britain and Argentina stop negotiating.	The charred remains of a British Sea King helicopter are found in Chile. Argentina claims to have captured 7 British SAS commandoes near Rio Gallegos City.			

All information derived from British sources.

Date	Negotiations/ Mediation	Military Operations	Internal Reaction		International Reaction
			Britain	Argentina	
21-5	Peru sends proposals to both countries to reopen negotiations.	British troops land at San Carlos and establish bridgehead. *HMS Ardent* is sunk, 1 destroyer and 3 frigates damaged and 2 helicopters lost. Argentina loses a total of 16 aircraft and 4 helicopters.			
22-5					The Soviet ambassador to the UN urges the Security Council to call for a ceasefire.
25-5		*HMS Coventry* and *Atlantic Conveyor* are sunk. Argentine mass attack on fleet and British bridgehead at San Carlos.		Argentine national day.	
28-5			The Pope arrives in London.		
29-5		The commander of the 2nd Battalion of the Parachute Regiment killed			

Date				
June 2-6	Perez de Cuellar recognizes that latest peace initiative has broken down.	during capture of Goose Green. Port Darwin also captured. 1600 Argentine soldiers captured. Heavy losses on both sides.	Major split in labour movement over position of parliamentary leadership.	
3-6	Panama and Spain produce resolutions at the UN calling for ceasefire; Britain vetos it; USA vetos it at first, subsequently amending this to an abstention.	British Vulcan makes forced landing in Rio de Janeiro. It is reported that Soviet technicians arrive in Argentina to install a protective radar net on the south coast.		Reagan and Mitterrand state their opposition to a total British victory. South Africa denies a reported secret pact with US and Britain to build a military base on Falklands.
4-6		Captain Astíz arrives in Britain as prisoner of war. France and Sweden demand to question him about disappearances of their nationals in Argentina.		
6-6			Polls show 80 per cent against the UN	European countries and Japan affirm

All information derived from British sources.

Date	Negotiations/Mediation	Military Operations	Internal Reaction		International Reaction
			Britain	**Argentina**	
6-6 contd.			holding the islands; 40 per cent for 'self-determination'.		support for Britain at Versailles summit.
7-6		Commander of Task Force appeals to Menendez to surrender.	Conservative spokesman talks about possible cost of the war — an estimated £1bn — to be paid by tax increases.	Galtieri says that Argentina will never accept a return to the *status quo* before 2 April.	
8-6	Thatcher says Britain will not return to UN to try to secure ceasefire. British troops advance over Falklands to the capital.	Liberian oil tanker bombed by unidentified aircraft outside exclusion zone. Argentina acknowledges 13 deaths and 3 missing since 20 May; Britain claims up to 60 Argentinians killed in the past week alone. *Sir Galahad* and *Sir Tristram* attacked; heavy British losses.	Reagan arrives in London and reaffirms full support for Thatcher.	The government releases 128 political prisoners.	
11-6				Pope arrives in Buenos Aires.	

98

Date					
12-6		British troops initiate final attack on Port Stanley.			All countries express satisfaction at the ending of bloodshed.
14-6 & 15-6		Argentine garrison surrender. A ceasefire is established over the islands. All Argentine troops captured.	All political party leaders congratulate Margaret Thatcher on the victory. British government says it will not negotiate with Argentina.	Demonstrations in Argentina blaming Galtieri. People ask for arms to continue the war: 'It's the end of a battle, not the end of the war', they say.	
16-6				Splits in the armed forces appear over how best to resolve the country's structural crisis. Galtieri forced out of office. Replaced provisionally as president by former Minister of the Interior, Alfredo Saint Jean, and as commander of the army by Gen. Cristino Nicolaides.	
17-6				Navy and air force, advocating a rapid return to civilian rule, withdraw from the	

All information derived from British sources.

Date	Negotiations/ Mediation	Military Operations	Internal Reaction		International Reaction
			Britain	**Argentina**	
				junta, leaving a₁my to consolidate power in an unstable government. Retired Gen. Reynaldo Bignone appointed president from 1 July, whilst Nicolaides retains command of army.	

100

5 Conclusion

The war in the South Atlantic cost the lives of more than a thousand people. To date it is estimated to have cost Britain £2 billion, with hundreds of millions more to be spent on the future defence of the islands. It has totally disrupted the economic and social life of the island community, and has stimulated a wave of jingoism and militarism in Britain. And all this has occurred when, according to the *Financial Times* of 7 April 1982, there was 'no vital national interest in any material or strategic sense' at stake and when the high-sounding moral principles that the politicians of all major parties assured us were at the root of the military adventure turn out to be hollow rhetoric. And worse, despite the bloodshed and huge expense, the problem of the status of the Falkland Islands and their future development has not been resolved.

Three main principles have been used to justify Britain's military action:

- That the Falklands are sovereign British territory and as such Britain had the legal right to defend them;
- That the Argentine invasion was an act of international aggression, which, if allowed to succeed, would have daunting implications for other territories faced with expansionist neighbours;
- That the Falkland Islanders had the right to self-determination in choosing to remain British.

Let us examine each of these arguments in turn.

British Sovereignty

Britain was clearly in full control of the islands until 2 April 1982 when Argentine forces invaded. Its claim to exercise sovereignty

101

A Just War?

'The argument to justify the action our country has taken is as follows: For one hundred and fifty years the Falkland Islands have been regarded under international law as a British possession. Unilateral annexation of them by armed invasion breaches international law and ignores the rights and repeatedly expressed wishes of the inhabitants. Such action is unacceptable both legally and morally.

In such a situation, the United Kingdom can claim the right to resist invasion. It can use the diplomatic, economic and, as a last resort, the military means necessary to uphold its legal rights.

It may well have an added responsibility to take action in so far as aggression often thrives on inaction and appeasement. Faced with aggression, it is not morally wrong to resist or to reassert rights with a measured degree of force.'

Basil Hume, Cardinal Archbishop of Westminster, 28 April 1982.

'Today, the scale and horror of modern warfare — whether nuclear or not — makes it totally unacceptable as a means of settling differences between nations. War should belong to the tragic past, to history. It should find no place on humanity's agenda for the future.'

Pope John Paul II, Coventry, 30 May 1982.

however, must be analysed from two points of view. Firstly, despite constant assurances from the Thatcher government that the British claim was irrefutable under international law, it is by no means certain that international courts would find in Britain's favour, as we have pointed out earlier. This fact has long been recognized by the British Foreign Office. As John Troutbeck, the head of the American Department in the Foreign Office, wrote in 1936:

The difficulty of the position is that our seizure of the Falkland Islands in 1833 was so arbitrary a procedure as judged by the ideology of the present day. It is therefore not easy to explain our possession without showing ourselves up as international bandits.

Won by conquest, the islands remained under British control to the dismay of successive Argentine governments of various political complexions. The strategic basis for the retention of the islands rested on Britain's economic dominance of Argentina until the 1940s. It was essential, therefore, that a settler population be supported in order for

Britain to continue to exert it claim. However, from our evidence, it is clear that successive British governments showed little interest in extending the islanders' political rights or improving their living standards.

Furthermore, economic arrangements were concluded with Argentina, which indicated Britain's inability to maintain the colony's viability without Argentine participation. Constant relegation of the dispute to the bottom of its in-tray indicated that even the Foreign Office saw the maintenance of the colony as an inconvenient aberration, a relic of past imperial adventures. With systematic decolonization having taken place elsewhere in the world, Britain's retention of an outpost in the South Atlantic is anachronistic. The failure to transfer sovereignty — or even to arrange partial solutions such as a Hong Kong-style leaseback arrangement — is interpreted in Latin America, by democrats as well as dictators, as unacceptable evidence of Britain's colonial profile.

A Stand Against International Aggression

The British government characterized the Argentine invasion of the Falkland Islands as an act of international aggression, and used this concept to mobilize wide domestic and international support for its military response. By invoking rhetoric about 'not appeasing dictators', and describing Margaret Thatcher's 'Churchillian resolve', parallels were drawn with Britain's role in World War Two. This made it easier to justify the dispatch of the task force in terms familiar to the generation which had been caught up in the struggle against fascism in the 1930s and 1940s.

In reality the Thatcher government cannot be acclaimed for its anti-fascism, or its opposition to dictatorship and repression in the Third World. Examples of this abound, particularly in Latin America, where support for Chile (restoration of diplomatic relations and trade), Argentina (arms sales) and El Salvador (observers sent to monitor elections which excluded the opposition) demonstrate the government's more usual stance. One of its first moves on coming to power was to wind down the programme which assisted opponents and victims of repression in Latin America to settle as refugees in Britain.

Yet the notion of Argentine aggression as a justification for Britains' military response remained a powerful factor. The task force was sent with broad opposition backing in parliament and the approval of a number of Commonweath countries. The Secretary-General of the Commonweath, a Guyanese national, in supporting the British stance, was mindful of the Venezuelan claim over a significant part of his country's territory. Similar fears that Guatemala might follow Argentina's example and invade Belize were expressed. The war also caused the postponement of Anglo-Spanish talks on the fate of Gibraltar. Britain continually played up the notion that Argentina's actions, if accepted by the international community, would set a precedent for the resolution by force of other disputes over sovereignty. Similar fears about West Berlin were raised in NATO and EEC circles. Domino theories abounded, fuelled by British apprehension that the last vestiges of its direct colonial control would be challenged elsewhere.

In utilizing accusations of Argentine aggression, Britain overlooked equivalent Argentine accusations that Britain's original invasion in 1833 and continued occupation of the islands constituted an act of international aggression. Furthermore, even though Argentina challenged Britain's conception of 'international law', which Britain claimed gave justification to its subsequent military actions, there is no reason to believe that Argentina would lose any case submitted to international arbitration.

The lesson for Argentina and the Third World is that for the foreseeable future their challenges to British power will be resisted wherever they may occur. The Falklands war proved that such challenges if they are to succeed have to be backed by superior and sophisticated weaponry and a sound economic infrastructure, which few Third World countries possess. For example, in 1980/81 Britain spent £10.78 billion on defence compared with Argentina's defence spending of £1.53 billion in 1980. The embellished accounts of British heroism should be seen in this context.

Far from refusing to appease dictators, Britain will continue to supply dictators and non-dictators alike with the arms they need to mount whatever aggression they choose. Britain's less than illustrious record of standing up to international aggression, even when its responsibility to do so has been enshrined in treaty (see box), and its continued support for some of the most unsavoury regimes in Latin America, make its pretensions to an international policing role highly discreditable.

Self-determination

The right of nations to self-determination is a widely-lauded principle. However, in relation to the Falkland Islands, the question of self-determination is highly problematic.

Firstly, whereas most of Britain's former colonies have vigorously campaigned for their independence, the Falkland Islanders have sought to retain their colonial relationship with Britain. This is partly because they are a settler population, and despite limitations placed on the rights of some of them to enter Britain, they do not claim a

Britain's Sorry Record

The appeal to high principles — democracy, self-determination, justice, expulsion of aggressors — which the British government used to rationalize going to war, is uncharacteristic of much of Britain's recent international practice. Citing some examples where Britain's behaviour clearly transgressed these high principles reveals that the racial identity of the Falkland Islanders was one of the factors which influenced Britain's decision to wage the war.

Diego Garcia

Leased to the United States for use as a nuclear base, Diego Garcia is a remote atoll in the middle of the Indian Ocean. Once part of Mauritius, it was detached before that country's independence in 1968 and remains a British colony to this day. For fourteen years Mauritius acquiesced to this, but in June 1982 a new government led by the *Mouvement Militant Mauricien* was overwhelmingly elected on a non-aligned socialist programme. It has made strong claims for the return of Diego Garcia to Mauritian sovereignty, hopes to remove the US base, and to join other Indian Ocean countries in declaring the area a 'zone of peace'.

When Nixon's Admiral Zumwalt went before the Senate Foreign Relations Committee in 1974 to obtain the funds for converting the island from a 'naval communications facility' to a full-scale base for housing a rapid deployment force, he told senators that the island was 'uninhabited'. The reason for this was that the population had been removed against its wishes by Britain and dumped on Mauritius without any support facilities in shantytowns and slums. Only in 1982, after eight hard years of lobbying, did the British government agree to pay the 1,200 exiled Diego Garcians £4 million as final compensation for their removal. This was done on the understanding that there would be no return to Diego Garcia. To date the United States has spent over £200 million constructing the base and has little intention of leaving it.

Zimbabwe

Rhodesian premier Ian Smith's illegal declaration of independence in Salisbury on 11 November 1965 constituted a revolt against British crown authority, and subverted the transition from minority to majority rule. The brutality and terror of Smith's rule sparked off a bitter civil war in which tens of thousands died over a period of fifteen years. The economies of the surrounding states were badly affected, and some suffered armed incursions by Smith's forces.

Much of this could have been averted had Britain intervened to protect the rights of the majority of its 5 million citizens in the territory in 1965. At the time the excuses of 'distance' and 'logistics' were used, but it should be remembered that Zimbabwe was a mere

105

5,000 miles distant, as opposed to the Falklands being 8,000 miles away. A further issue was whether Britain's military forces could be mobilized against its so-called 'kith and kin', the white settlers. Racial solidarity with the white minority prevailed, and put paid to the use of armed force. Instead economic sanctions were imposed; yet, towards the end of the war it was revealed that major British companies such as Shell and BP had never implemented sanctions. Their oil supplies prolonged Smith's rule, strengthening his forces in the war.

Cyprus

In 1960, Britain, Greece and Turkey signed a Treaty of Guarantee in London to protect the sovereign integrity of the new Republic of Cyprus in the eastern Mediterranean. The treaty obliged the three powers to consult in the event of any threat to Cyprus's independence. In 1967 the CIA assisted right-wing Greek colonels to take power in Athens. This junta favoured 'enosis', the unity of Cyprus with Greece, and encouraged right-wing Greek Cypriots to stage a coup on 15 July 1974. The coup immediately threw Cypriot independence into jeopardy.

The Turkish prime minister Bulent Ecevit flew to London to persuade the British government to intervene jointly in Cyprus as guarantors. Britain's failure to respond precipitated a unilateral Turkish invasion, the effective partition of the island and massive population displacement and refugee problems. It seems clear that Britain had a legal duty to intervene as a guarantor power to re-establish the *status quo*. Furthermore its military occupation of 99 square miles of the island as 'sovereign bases' made it feasible to intervene.

Instead, Britain's inaction contributed to the profound problems faced by the Cypriot people in the aftermath of the island's partition, and has led to the further destabilization of a very vulnerable part of the world.

Banaba

In 1948 the inhabitants of the Pacific island of Banaba were removed by Britain and resettled in Fiji so that the British Phosphate Commission could strip-mine the wealthy phosphate deposits on the island. In the interim the ecology of the island has been damaged so badly that human habitation is virtually impossible.

£60 million worth of phosphates have been exported from Banaba, with almost no royalties accruing to its original inhabitants. This compares unfavourably with the fate of the other phosphate island in the Pacific, Nauru, which after independence from Australia in 1968, enjoyed a per capita income of £1,500 per year on the strength of royalties.

In the longest civil action in British legal history (1971-76), the 3,100 islanders sued the Commission for compensation, refusing a derisory offer of £0.8 million. The outcome of the case was an award of £9,000 to the islanders, which did not even cover the £300,000 incurred in legal costs. The court absolved the British government from legal responsibility for past instances of colonial exploitation.

Public pressure caused the Foreign Secretary of the time, Dr David Owen, to offer the islanders an ex-gratia payment of £6.5 million (equivalent to £200 per year for each islander). In the words of Sir Bernard Braine MP, 'Ironically Dr Owen's offer is only giving back to the islanders a small proportion of their own money which was filched from them over a long period. This is the last act in a shameful story of exploitation.'

But there was to be a further disappointment for the Banabans. Against their will, their island was included in the indepence package for the Gilbert Islands, now Kiribati, which has jurisdiction over the spending of all taxes and royalties accruing from Banaba's phosphates.

---

separate nationality or identity as a distinct nation. The absence of a democratic process on the islands, determined largely by the level of paternalism and company monopoly, holds out little promise for the development of popular self-determination.

Yet the islanders' desire to remain British is the sticking point in any agreement which Britain might earlier have concluded with Argentina. Rather than offer options such as resettlement with compensation, and an end to discrimination under the Nationality Act, Britain staged a costly war under the guise of protecting these sentiments.

By doing so, the rights of the islanders were declared paramount. Not only did this conflict with the rights of 27 million Argentinians, but the phenomenal cost of the war — £1 million per islander — was given precedence over the claims of other groups of British citizens to their national resources. Few of Britain's three million unemployed will ever have access to £1 million to guarantee their right to work. Few of the homeless or inadequately housed, or those without proper social services, education and health care have been so liberally bestowed with the resources needed to guarantee their rights.

Had the crisis been resolved through a transfer of sovereignty, the islanders would have had to balance their desire to remain British with their desire to remain on the islands. Possibilities might then have been discussed for schemes such as limited autonomy for the islands, dual nationality for their inhabitants and other forms of protection of minority rights. However, the war has polarized positions on both sides, leaving little room for any peaceful resolution of the conflict.

The ultimate irony came after the fighting had ceased, when the British government made it quite clear that the self-determination of the islanders was not a paramount concern of theirs. Within two days of the Argentine surrender at Port Stanley, the British Foreign Secretrary, Francis Pym, stated that the islanders did not have the right of veto over future British policy. In theory, sovereignty could be transferred to Argentina despite the islanders' objections, once more exposing the myth of self-determination.

Imperial Britain

From the outset of the recent conflict, the British government and the media were at pains to point out that the Argentine invasion of the Falklands was undertaken to diffuse the rapidly growing domestic hostility towards the military government in Buenos Aires. Recuperation of the Malvinas was probably the only issue that could unite the left and the right in Argentina. Seen in the context of British instransigence over the years of negotiations, retaking the islands was indeed a universally popular crusade.

However, this same argument can also be used to explain the British response. The government was clearly facing a difficult time at home: an economic recession that refused to 'bottom out', unemployment levels unheard of since the 1930s, polarization in the inner cities and a gradual loss of support to the newly-formed centrist Social Democrat Party. It is in this context that the government's exaggerated respose must be analysed.

The Thatcher government draws its ideological support from the far right of the Conservative Party. Her most loyal supporters are those who approve of her hard line attitudes to the trade unions, her views on law and order, and her efforts to maintain an imperial role for Britain, by large increases in defence spending. Her 'iron maiden' image is one on which she has capitalized. It was to this group of hard-line right-wing Conservatives that Mrs Thatcher had to report that Britain had been caught napping by a 'second rate Latin American dictator'. Not only had her government been humiliated, but that humiliation was due at least in part to its own incompetence in reading the numerous signals emanating from Buenos Aires that indicated all was not well. Even reports from the captain of the *HMS Endurance* that an invasion was imminent were ignored by the Foreign Office, and Mrs Thatcher was firm in her belief a few days before the Argentine invasion that 42 marines were a 'sufficient deterrent against any possible aggression'.

The crisis therefore hit at the very root of the Thatcher ideology. Why spend millions of pounds on defence if Britain cannot defend herself? What price an 'iron maiden' who can so easily be upstaged by a Third World dictator? After all, Jimmy Carter's attempts to stage an Israeli-style raid on Teheran to release captive US embassy officials had aborted, costing him a second term as president.

Similarly, the future of the Thatcher government was clearly threatened, not from an onslaught by the left, but from the hard right of the Conservative Party. Mrs Thatcher moved quickly to secure her support. Her government's incompetence had to be paid for. The right put the blame on the Foreign Office, which led the Foreign Secretary, Lord Carrington, and two of his ministers to resign from office. Then Britain's humiliation had to be avenged: hence the sending of the task force. The depth of British military tradition, the ingrained imperialism, shocking to many who had not perceived it before, fuelled the rush to war. National pride swelled: Britain might not be able to solve the problems of domestic unemployment, or the violence of the inner cities, but by jingo she could and would do something about the Falklands!

If by-election and local election results at the time of the conflict are an indication of political fortunes, Mrs Thatcher reaped the benefits from the arousal of so much chauvinism. The Conservative Party's popularity rating increased as the battle over the Falklands intensified. Public support for the military action continued as the media incessantly expounded the government's rationale for the adventure, despite the casualties and evident cost. The efficiency with which the government mobilized the media in the face of the 'national emergency' and the media's acquiescence, whether self-imposed or at the hands of the Ministry of Defence censor (described by the Independent Television News task force correspondent as 'rigid, unreasonable and stupid') have far-reaching implications for the ways in which 'public opinion' is constructed (see appendix on the press). Voiced opposition to the war was very limited. Few in the Conservative Party opposed the Thatcher line. Even those who saw the task force as a threat to British economic links with Latin America (and indeed with other Third World countries), either left silently (as in the case of Lord Carrington) or refused to take on their belligerent colleagues. Yet the *Financial Times*, which represents the views of a large section of British capital, was clearly opposed to the task force from the outset. They clearly put Britain's economic interests in Latin America before the nationalist rhetoric of the government.

Opposition from the Labour Party was also limited. The party leadership continually stressed the importance of negotiations through the United Nations in attempting to avert the war but at the same time supported the sending of the task force. Its position claimed some basis on the party manifesto which stated that under no circumstances would the Falkland Islands be handed over to any Argentine regime which violated human and civil rights. In the belief that economic and political sanctions coupled with military threats would not have been effective, the party leadership argued that there was no alternative but to support the government in sending in the task force. They argued that this position supported United Nations resolution 502 and amounted to a firm stand against international aggression and a fascist Latin American regime and supported the rights of the islanders to self-determination. More sustained Labour opposition to the sending of the task force and the pursuit of war was limited to a group of 37 MPs and some constituency parties.

The position adopted by the Labour Party raises three questions however. The first concerns the role of the United Nations in the dispute. The oft-quoted UN Security Council resolution 502 has three parts. It called for:

- an immediate cessation of hostilities,
- the withdrawal of military forces, and
- negotiations between Britain and Argentina on the question of sovereignty over the islands.

It is clear that Argentina did not abide by the first two parts of the resolution. However, the sending of the British task force and the refusal to negotiate the question of sovereignty over the islands with Argentina did not support the British claim that they were abiding by the resolution. Paradoxically, while in April the resolution's call for a withdrawal of military forces was favourable to Britain, by June the same resolution gave some support to Argentina in the face of the British proposal to garrison the islands.

The second question concerns the alternative stategies available to Britain after 2 April 1982. The Labour Party leadership's acceptance of the Thatcher policy meant that it offered no public challenge to the government strategy in the House of Commons, thus pre-empting wider debate and consultation within the party on possible alternatives. Critical MPs were isolated. Labour's leaders refused the offer of consultation with Argentine trade unionists when the latter hinted at their possibility. Even a NATO package of full sanctions was never openly discussed as a potential alternative to the task force. Mrs Thatcher's claim that 'there is no alternative', heard in the past in relation to her economic policy, was never challenged.

The third point concerned the nature of the Argentine government that led the nation to war. It was widely suggested that a strong British military response to the invasion was in some way supporting those struggling for political and social change within Argentina. Unfortunately for those in Britain who held this view, the Argentinian trade unionists, church activists and human rights workers who led the opposition to the military government in Buenos Aires did not agree.

All of them have consistently supported the Argentine claim to the Malvinas and the vast majority supported the invasion. They universally deplored the sending of the British task force. They argued that real support for their cause would have come previously from ceasing to sell arms to the junta, international support for their human rights campaign, and most importantly, a rapid settlement to the Malvinas dispute, so that successive military governments could not use this unifying issue to divert popular opinion every time they faced internal criticism.

International Implications

By embarking on the war, Britain has done significant damage to its relations with Latin America. Apart from a few states which feared that their neighbours would resort to military solutions of territorial disputes, most Latin American countries backed Argentina and rejected Britain's maintenance of a colony in the South Atlantic. Backing for Argentina came from governments as diverse as Guatemala and Nicaragua, Brazil and Cuba. Latin America perceived the conflict as a North-South problem, as the re-assertion of alien colonialism which was therefore to be opposed irrespective of the political nature of the Argentine regime.

No attempt was made by the British government to utilize the dispute to think again and build new bridges with the Third World, or to display a more acceptable image. Instead Britain reaffirmed its imperial role. Thatcher, addressing thousands of Conservative faithfuls at Cheltenham racecourse on 5 July 1982, declared 'that the Falklands triumph had proved that Britons were still the same people who had built an Empire, and had ruled a quarter of the world'. Such statements can only confirm on Britain the hostility of many people around the world who have struggled against colonial subjugation.

Thatcher's attempts to refloat colonialism have a number of other consequences. Mass unemployment, de-industrialization, inner city rebellion and the dismantling of the public sector have been the result of high unpopular monetarist policies. The war has been the only project put forward by the Conservatives around which they have been able to build a national consensus. In the public sector strikes of mid-1982, Thatcher has appealed to the workers to uphold the 'spirit of the South Atlantic' and to abandon industrial action for ostensibly more patriotic gestures. The themes of national pride, singleminded action and heroic triumph are all being invoked by Thatcher in order to win a second term of office.

In practical terms, the losers are the British banks and subsidiaries

111

which will close, the exporters who will lose contracts, the universities which will fail to attract students, and the human rights and solidarity groups whose work the war will have made more difficult. And because of Latin America's backing of Argentina, these British losses may extend to the rest of the continent for some considerable time to come.

In a recent Latin America Bureau publication, *The European Challenge* (1982), we pointed to the new relationship which Western European countries were attempting to forge with Latin America, acting as a counterweight to the influence of the United States. Since the war, however, the confidence with which Europe had adopted its new role has been severely shaken. It was clear from the hesitancy with which Britain's European partners supported the task force that they saw their Latin American interests in danger.

Sanctions were grudgingly applied by the European Economic Community (EEC) with Ireland and Italy refusing to renew them after the first month, and the other members planning to lift them as soon as hostilities formally ceased. The fact that the EEC cooperated with Britain at all was a result of intra-community politics. The effective *quid pro quo* was the abandonment of the Luxemburg Compromise which had allowed Britain to veto EEC farm pricing policies. It can be argued that this was a far greater blow to British sovereignty than the Argentine invasion of the Falklands. Simultaneously, the EEC member states made it clear that their support for sanctions was of a limited and temporary nature. Spain, currently a member of the UN Security Council, had only abstained on resolution 502 because of its application to join both NATO and the EEC; its opposition to Britain over the Falklands and Gibraltar would otherwise have caused it to vote against the resolution.

Europe's less than wholehearted response was initially matched by that of the United States. During the first month of the conflict, while the task force was on its way to the South Atlantic, President Reagan attempted to pacify both parties in the spirit of Pax Americana. Secretary of State Alexander Haig was sent on a long-distance triangular mediation mission. However, with the retaking of South Georgia, Haig's efforts collapsed, and after 30 April the US swung behind Britain. This decision marked a victory for those in the Reagan administration who argued that the main threat to the US came from the Soviet Union. The logic of this position dictated the need to support NATO allies in any conflict, and elevated the North Atlantic alliance above any commitment to Argentina.

This was to prove damaging to United States foreign policy in Latin America in two respects. On the one hand it seriously affected the ideological basis of the inter-American state system carefully

Strategies for the South Atlantic

On 24 May 1982 the South African press revealed that a DC-8 aircraft belonging to Cargolux of Luxemburg, and leased to Aero Uruguay, had been loading crates labelled 'tractor parts' destined for Argentina. The crates were believed to contrain Israeli-made aircraft drop tanks. Israel was probably using South Africa as a trans-shipment route because of the friendly relations which existed between the military sectors of both countries and the Argentine junta. Although South Africa made a point of remaining 'neutral' during the Falklands war, its close working relationship with the Argentine military should not be overlooked.

This relationship has been cultivated assidously since the late 1960s. Twenty-five years before the outbreak of the Falklands war, Britain surrended control over its major naval base in the South Atlantic, Simonstown, to South Africa's jurisdiction. Agreements were signed for joint UK-South African use of the base so as to patrol the strategic Cape sea route, around which most of the oil supplies for Europe travel. However, under international pressure against collaboration with apartheid, Britain withdrew from the Simonstown Agreement and the naval base in 1976.

Yet the North Atlantic Treaty Organization (NATO) countries were still very keen to ensure that the Cape route remained free from potential Soviet interference, especially during and after the 1975 Angolan independence war. When South Africa built its enormous Silvermine maritime communications centre near Simonstown, NATO set up channels whereby naval intelligence communications could be exchanged with South Africa. During the Falklands war, for example, Silvermine provided Britain with information on two Angola-based Soviet Bear spy-planes which were keeping watch on the naval task force.

Although NATO has an 'Atlantic Command', its area of operation is strictly confined to the North Atlantic. No equivalent organization exists for the South Atlantic, although there has often been speculatiuon about the formation of a South Atlantic Treaty Organization (SATO) aligned to NATO. This speculation grew as Pretoria's relations with Latin America increased from the late 1960s. Trade quadrupled between 1966-77, and diplomatic relations were established with 12 Latin American states. Pretoria began to see Latin America as a potential military ally, a source and market for arms and a mutually reinforcing ideological bedfellow.

This rapproachement suited the NATO countries in defence terms. Extension of NATO's field of operations was out of the question, and Britain's role in the area had diminished, but the potential existed for the South Atlantic nations themselves to operate some form of defence system in the area. Such a scheme was consonant with the 'Nixon doctrine', whereby the United States aimed at building up a series of military allies in the Third World which would act out a regional policing role. Positive encouragement was given to the Latin American navies in a series of joint manoeuvres with the US navy (UNITAS exercises) during this time.

South Africa also stepped up its overtures towards the juntas, and premier Vorster dispatched his foreign minister Hilgard Müller on two major visits to Latin America in 1969 and 1973. These visits stimulated a greater degree of military collaboration, especially with Argentina. During the latter visit, the newly elected Peronist vice-president, Dr Vicente Solano Lima, pledged to strengthen ties with South Africa: 'We are not interested in how the South Africa government came to power, nor in the social situation in the country. We are only interested in tightening still further the links between us.' Naval visits, exchanges of attachés, and offers of equipment all took place. *Time* magazine reported Argentina's willingness to sell its counter-insurgency aircraft, the Pucará, to South Africa, in March 1975.

The appointment in 1980 of Rear-Admiral Ruben Chamorro as naval attaché in South Africa indicates a significant upgrading of the naval mission. Since 1968, Buenos Aires had only appointed officers above the rank of captain to posts in Washington and London. Specialist training courses were provided for Argentine officers in South Africa, and in 1981, General Mario Benjamin Menendez — Argentina's chief of staff and later governor of the Malvinas — visited South Africa and was treated with great warmth and enthusiasm by its naval establishment.

Military relations with Chile have also improved, with South Africa appointing its second-ranking general, John Dutton, as its first ambassador to Santiago in December 1980. South Africa now possesses the world's tenth largest arms industry, and has sold at least 12 'Cactus' missiles (France's 'Crotale' built under licence) to Chile. Apart from Taiwan, Chile was the only country to participate in the apartheid republic's twentieth anniversary celebrations. The training ship *Esmeralda*, notorious for its use as a torture-chamber for pro-Allende sailors after the *coup* in 1973, was sent on a courtesy mission. Chilean sailors goose-stepped on a parade through Durban and impressed South African officials with a rendering of the national anthem in Afrikaans. Earlier in 1981, the chief of the Chilean navy, Admiral José Merino Castro, a member of Pinochet's junta, led an official delegation to South Africa.

Yet despite the intensification of bilateral naval relations, SATO has never materialized. Brazil — whose participation would be a key to the treaty's success — has been unwilling to involve itself. It prefers to cultivate good relations with other African states (particularly the oil producers, Nigeria, Angola and Libya), often denouning apartheid, and favouring the independence of Namibia under SWAPO, the territory's liberation movement. Rivalry between Argentina and Chilean navies over the possession of islands in the Beagle Channel has also put paid to their collaboration in a defence arrangement in the South Atlantic.

However the idea refuses to die. On coming to power the Reagan administration hosted top-level delegations from all the states concerned and gave backing — through the presence of its roving ambassador, General Vernon Walters — to an important privately sponsored conference on strategy in the South Atlantic in Buenos Aires in June 1981 where the question of SATO was thoroughly discussed. More recently, Margaret Thatcher's suggestion that the UK, US, Brazil and other states should use the recaptured Falklands as an international naval base, is little more than an attempt to gain international backing for Britain's continued military retention of the islands. In view of the war, and the reluctance of the US to alienate its Latin American-allies further, Thatchers's idea is politically impracticable.

Although the idea of a South Atlantic pact will continue to be raised, it seems unlikely to materialize in the forseeable future. Instead we can expect the strengthening of a looser network of bilateral military, economic and diplomatic links between South Africa and its friends across the South Atlantic.

constructed by the United States since the Second World War, to which there had been three cornerstones: the Monroe Doctrine, dating from 1823, which sought to exclude European powers from the American continent and thereby establish US hegemony in the region; the 1947 Rio Treaty — the Inter-American Treaty of Reciprocal Assistance — which established a collective security doctrine by which any American state threatened by an outside power could call on fellow signatories to the treaty for military assistance; and finally, the creation in 1948 of the Organization of American States (OAS). The OAS traditionally acted in line with US foreign policy in the region and was used on several occasions to legitimate direct US intervention (as in Guatemala in 1954 and the Dominican Republic in 1965) or political pressure (as with Cuba's expulsion from the OAS in 1962 and subsequent economic sanctions). By the late 1970s, as numerous Latin American states sought to assert a more independent line from that of the US, the OAS opposed any US intervention against the Sandinista government in Nicaragua (1979).

US prestige suffered a more serious blow on 29 May 1982, as a result of the Falklands crisis, when OAS foreign ministers passed a resolution which denounced the US for having violated both the Charter of the OAS and the Rio Treaty. The resolution demanded that Washington lift all coercive measures against Argentina and refrain from providing material assistance to Britain. Condemning the British task force, they called on OAS members to provide assistance to

Argentina. With abstentions from only four countries (the US itself, Colombia, Chile and Trinidad & Tobago), Latin America made it clear that US influence in the organization had been reduced. Peru's former foreign minister, José de la Puente Radbill, stated that US actions had 'completely broken the inter-American system' and endangered the future of the OAS. It has been openly suggested that the US be excluded from the OAS, or that the OAS be disbanded in favour of strengthening SELA (the Latin American Economic System) of which the US is not a member.

Countries such as Venezuela and Brazil, both close to Washington in the past, distanced themselves as a result of the crisis. President Figueiredo of Brazil cut short an official visit to Washington. In the same vein, Peru, which had initially offered to mediate in the crisis in conjunction with Dr Javier Perez de Cuellar, the UN Secretary-General, backed the Argentine position once Washington became commited to supporting London. Only Chile, in dispute with Argentina over the Beagle Channel Islands, failed to offer Buenos Aires clear support, and seems to have been a secret staging post for certain British military operations.

The Falklands war thus gave Latin America the opportunity to test its relations with the United States. A clear alignment with Argentina would have affirmed that the US' commitment to inter-American solidarity was a serious one. Instead, Latin American states received confirmation that the US was only interested in a hegemonic role in the Americas, and was unprepared to defend Argentina against an extra-hemispheric enemy.

Paradoxically, this US position dealt the second major blow to the Reagan administration's policy in Latin America. On coming to office Reagan made it clear that his government would oppose the popular guerrilla forces in El Salvador and Guatemala. In the case of El Salvador, the US offered training, arms and advisers to the government's military forces. However, the extent of US involvement was curbed by Congress, and has attracted the hostility of many Americans, as well as opposition from the governments of Mexico, France and other countries.

In order to justify further intervention, the US turned to the OAS for backing for its Central American policy. Although OAS support for the Duarte government in El Salvador was forthcoming, no multi-lateral intervention force was established. Yet the Argentine junta responded most enthusiastically and dispatched counter-insurgency forces to Central America. Now, however, the US stand over the Falklands has put an end to Argentina's willingness to act as Washington's proxy in Central America, and has caused it to increased its prominence in the non-aligned movement. The war has meant that the United States will have to look to other strategies to achieve its aims in El Salvador and Guatemala.

Indeed, the war brought to the fore conflicts within the US foreign policy-making establishment. Disagreements between Alexander Haig (pro-NATO) and Jeane Kirkpatrick (a Latin Americanist) surfaced in a key note in the UN Security Council on 3 June 1982, when at Kirkpatrick's insistence, the US' support for the British veto of a ceasefire resolution proposed by Spain and Panama changed to a position of abstention. This disagreement was one of the factors which culminated in the resignation of Haig as Secretary of State at the end of the same month.

Finally, one of the chief implications of the crisis arises from the use of force by both parties in the pursuit of their policies. The elevation of military solutions above diplomacy and negotiation, the devaluation of multilateral arenas for resolving disputes, and triumph/defeat based less on international justice than on superior/inferior might, all contribute to the reduction of chances for the peaceful settlement of future international disputes. The war allowed the testing of a new generation of weapons and raised sales of those which, like the Exocet missile, proved to be effective. This too had the effect of increasing the worldwide investment in warfare as a realistic policy option.

Options for the Future

Both economically and politically, the immediate future of the Falkland Islands looks very bleak. Officially Britain is tentatively considering three alternative proposals for the islands:
- independence, giving executive and legislative power to the islanders with Britain guaranteeing the islands' integrity (a Cyprus-style arrangement);
- associated statehood, whereby the Queen remains head of state, but all matters of government except foreign policy and defence would be decided by the islanders; and finally:
- self-government, which has as yet not been clearly defined.

None of these proposals, however, face the central issue, namely how to resolve the dispute with Argentina. If Argentina is not party to any proposed solution, there can be no guarantee of stability and, therefore, of economic development on the islands. The British government's present attitude towards Argentina remains instransigent. Argentina will not be involved in negotiations in the foreseeable future, and Britain will defend the islands militarily against any Argentine attempts to recapture them. The idea of 'Fortress Falklands' summarises the present position.

DAILY EXPRESS
THE VOICE OF BRITAIN

━━INVASION OF THE FALKLAND ISLANDS━━

:Our loyal subjects

We MUST defend them

EXPRESS OPINION

INCOMPETENT

FULL STORY OF THE FALKLANDS CRISIS: SEE PAGES 2, 3, 6, 7 AND 9

Daily Mail

GRAND NATIONAL

Falklands fiasco leaves Government facing crisis Commons today

SHAMED!

Under the flag of occupation

BY GORDON GREIG and JOHN DICKIE

Reporting with a gun held in my back

BY WILLIAM LANGLEY

DAILY Mirror

GRAND NATIONAL FENCE BURNED

4 PAGE AINTREE PULL-OUT: SEE PAGE 19

PRISONERS OF WAR

40 British warships on Falklands standby

CHELSEA SOCCER CLUB SOLD SEE BACK PAGE

BINGO £600,000 MUST BE WON!

Sun

GRAND NATIONAL

Special crisis issue

BATTLE FOR THE ISLANDS

IT'S WAR!

- 40 warships ready
- Paras are called up
- Prince Andy to go

FULL STORY: PAGES 2, 3, 4, 5 & 6

Appendix: Public Opinion, the Popular Press and the Organization of Ideas

*Many people have remarked on the type of coverage the war in the South Atlantic received at the hands of the popular press. In this special contribution to the book, **Patricia Holland**, who has studied and written on the role of the popular press, argues that behind the banner headlines and sensational pictures there lies a coherent ideology that plays an important role in forming people's ideas.*

The departure of the task force ('Sailing to salvage Britain's pride', *Mirror*), the sinking of the General Belgrano ('Gotcha', *Sun*), the capture of South Georgia ('Quick fire marines grab penguin isle', *Star*), the return of the QE2 ('sexy Jane . . . spilled the beans on the saucy antics that turned the QE2 into a love nest', *Sun*), the attack on Port Stanley ('Our boys caught Argies napping', *News of the World*); striking front pages; double page spreads with dramatic photographs, giant lettering and graphic devices held in a mosaic lay-out; these are the celebratory set pieces at which our mass circulation tabloids excel. These displays are not to be read in a linear fashion but are to be appreciated whole, sampled, a caption here a paragraph there. The mode of appreciation is visual as much as verbal.

Laced with jokes and charged with emotion, geared to arouse anger, pity, desire, this vivid and compulsive style is closer to that of cartoon comics than it is to the literary sequences of the *Times* or the *Guardian*. It is the declared intent of the popular papers to entertain. Indeed, it is necessary for them to achieve a dramatic impact in their news and feature pages if those pages are to hold their own in their internal competition with the advertisements which ensure their

119

War Comic illustration.

Guardian 26 May 1982.

survival. And, as far as the popular press is concerned, what could be more entertaining that a war? The genre is well established in other media, war films and boys' comics; the imagery, the characters and the plot lines are already familiar to generations of males from the age of eight upwards.

At the level of boys' comics the notorious *Sun* headlines, 'Stick it up your junta', 'Wallop', 'We'll smash 'em', fall naturally into place. And the stress on hardware, on the technology of war, seems just as natural. We are offered silhouettes of the different types of battleship, diagrams of weapons ('the deadly missile that skims the sea at almost the speed of sound and strikes from 20 miles away' *Sun* 5 May), photographs of helicopters taking off, jets in mid-flight, exploding bombs and burning ships. The photographs of people stress an action-man image like that of the heroes rushing up the beach with guns at the ready used once in *The Sun* and twice in the *Daily Mirror* on Saturday 3 April, the day of the emergency meeting of parliament, before the decision to send the task force had formally been announced. It was a picture of marines on routine duty in the Falklands, and strictly bore a decorative rather than an illustrative relation to the story, which, in fact announced the Argentine take over. But it carried the flavour of invasion and anticipated the desired British response. Stylished figures from this picture were used in all the popular papers over the following weeks as a symbol of the conflict. Later on we were shown the Special Boat Squadron, who can see at night, who kill with their bare hands and are also electronic marvels. 'They'll come home a lot leaner and a bit meaner' (*Mail* 11 May).

So these are 'times when men walk tall' (*Express* 30 April), and, in true comic book style the heroes of war are named and celebrated. There's Admiral Sandy, 'the man England expects to win' (*Express* 30

April), 'this quietly spoken man is ruthless in action' (*Sun* 26 April); then there's the bewhiskered Cap'n Birdseye who went down with his ship. 'Farewell old seadog', cried *The Sun* (28 May). There's the serious professional Bertie Penfold, 'the man with a place in history' (*Mail* 4 May). He was the first pilot to shoot down an Argentine plane, pictured in all the papers posing in front of the Harrier which carries his name. Finally, as the war progressed, there came the eulogies of the war reporter as hero. 'The incomparable Max' Hastings, for example, a man who, we're told, sits casually on a shooting stick and smokes a Havana cigar while reporting a battle (*Express* 9 June).

And it is thus, woven into all this myth making and story telling, that a series of organizing ideas are brought into play, a range of concepts mobilized, which mark out for readers possible ways of thinking about the crisis. It has been pointed out how news from the Falklands has been managed, filtered and timed by the Ministry of Defence, (*Guardian* 8 June; *Observer* 9 May). But, quite apart from a consideration of the truth or falsehood of each report or picture, it is this use of language, choice of pictures, and arrangement of stories into a daily comic strip narrative with colourful characters and a developing plot which offers a compelling framework for those organizing ideas, those central ideological themes.

The relation of the media to public opinion is a problematic one. Do they influence it, reflect it, reflect back what they themselves have first constructed . . . ? The issues are complex, for, to a certain extent, the press must do all of those things. Yet how do we know about public opinion apart from the media's own reports? The popular papers, indeed, construct 'public opinion' as one of the characters in their

121

drama. It becomes a kind of affirmative Greek chorus, a crowd which occasionally troops onto stage to offer patriotic support to 'the nation' and 'our boys'. 'I must go back and talk to them', cried Margaret Thatcher when the Argentine surrender was announced, and the picture shows her receiving the crowd's ecstatic greeting (*Mail* 15 June). Inside the same paper a feature article assures us that, 'Every back in Britain is a little bit straighter today' and that our second best status, exemplified by 'tea slopped into the saucer by slatterns in dirty overalls' has been overcome. Peter Jenkins in the *Guardian* reached a similar conclusion, expressed rather more discreetly: 'Patriotic instincts have been aroused, and they potentially transcend the dividing lines of class and ideology' (16 June).

This mixture of appeal to public opinion, assertions about public opinion, and the weaving of 'public opinion' into the narrative is powerful and convincing. Thus actual public opinion is offered easy channels to flow along. Possible words for us to use, possible ways to link our ideas, come easily to hand. At the same time dissident opinions are either excluded or rendered contemptible. Thus the newspapers organize and give power to the opinions they represent, while leaving actual dissent without a public voice and without a public language.

We have seen the boys' comic relish for warfare for its own sake, the celebration of the instruments of war and the characters required by war. As well as creating heroes on 'our' side, this approach creates an enemy who is both vicious and contemptible. The British flag in the Falklands was 'hauled down by an inferior power' (*Express* 3 April),

122

whose leader Galtieri, is a 'vainglorious incompetant man' (*Express* 4 May). Such sentiments draw on the racism never far beneath the surface of the popular press. On 4 May, William Hickey reported on the patriotic songs he had been sent — at his own invitation. On reading them 'I felt like shaking my fist at anyone looking vaguely Latin' (*Express*). This adds a sense of invulnerability to 'our side', who are somehow protected by their moral rightness. 'The right is on our side, so is the might' (*Express* 30 April). So when we suffer losses it comes as a shock, and the sense of outrage and thirst for revenge is the greater.

The theme of 'law and order' has been a point of reference from the beginning, together with its associated notion of the inviolability of private property. 'There's a robber in one of our houses who must be ejected' (*Express* 3 April); 'Argentina has stolen our territory' (*Sun* 26 April). As time went by 'we' (the British) changed from being outraged property owners to becoming 'we' the police force, brought in, as they so often are, to control unruly of subversive groups.

Many of these themes, like racism, law and order and private ownership, are organized around the central, basic idea of 'nation'. The *Daily Express* habitually describes itself as 'the voice of Britain', and, apart from the *Mirror*, all the popular papers have hastened to claim that unitary voice. Dissent, or even hesitation, is ruled out as 'treacherous' (*Sun* 11 May). The idea of 'nation', of the British as a nation including us all, inevitably united behind the government and behind 'our boys', is a basic assumpton behind the style of the reporting and of the imagery. Since the *Mirror*, too, operates within this same framework of assumptions, it was led into many ambiguities of style.

So, a guide-book version of British history is summoned up, 'the navy sets out to win back Britain's pride' (*Sun* 6 April), Churchill and Nelson are wheeled on stage and the Union Jack flaps triumphantly through the photographs. Soldiers, politicians and reporters become part of a chorus of assent, and the language of the newspapers co-opts the readers, too. Are we not all part of 'Britain'? It was 'our' territory that was invaded, 'our' rights which were violated. This distant invasion became in the *Mirror*, 'the peril that faces Britain' (26 April). *The Sun* demanded 'where would our people be safe in the world? What part of our possessions . . . would be secure?' (6 April) and, in the *Mail* Paul Johnson spoke of 'what the nation will demand', and assured us that 'the losses we are asked to accept will reinforce the determination to uphold the rule of law and the fundamental decencies of civilization' (5 May). Mrs Thatcher herself recognised the ideological power of the word 'we'.

The idea of 'nation', of course, clouds over any divisions within a country. Class and gender fall into place as natural divisions and we are left with no language to distinguish between the British government and various segments of the British people, nor the Argentine government and the Argentinian people. *The Sun* uses 'junta' to imply all Argentinians; its 'stick it up your junta' jibes are directed as much at drowning Argentine sailors as at the admirals and generals who commanded them. However, the popular newspapers have suddenly discovered that Argentina is a fascist dictatorship, and blatantly assert that 'Britain does not appease dictators' (*Express* 8 April). Where convenient they point to the fact that the Argentinian army includes 'poignantly vulnerable conscripts' (*Mail* 10 June), but the *Mail* in particular has somehow managed to imply that the evilness of the government invokes the compliance of the people it suppresses. In a feature on 7 May, V.S. Naipaul describes a 'nation of strutting machoes' 'a society spewing on itself'. A leader on the 5 May spoke of the 'military dictatorship backed by a passionately patriotic Argentine people', and on the 4 May we were told that those people 'patriotically will themselves to accept the propaganda they're fed'. Nevertheless the *Mail* in particular never allows us to forget who the real enemy is; 'Marxist dictatorships go further in ruthless control of life and thought than any military junta' (10 June).

Finally, how does the war affect the presentation of the relations between the sexes — a theme which is in all circumstances a constant obsession with the popular press. Well, they tell us that just as war comics are for boys, so wars are for men. 'Men like to fight and are excited by the prospect of battle' declares Peter McKay (*Express* 30

April). A war like this one marks out a suitable range of relationships between men and women.

As the task force left England the papers were full of weeping mothers, wives and girl friends. Women's role is to weep and to accept. A mother who questioned whether her son should go was severely reprimanded by Jean Rook (*Express* 7 April). The difference between male and female is here presented at its most extreme. Joe Ashton, the voice of the people, remembers that soldiers at war think only of three things 'Crumpet, grub and crumpet' (*Star* 26 April), and the *Sun* sees itself as serving that need (30 April). In case we miss the point Peter McKay sums it up for us, 'Cut the girl talk, this is war. In these times when men walk tall . . . there has been a small outbreak of nostalgia for men as brutes . . . Right now it must be quite hard to be a feminist.' (*Express* 30 April). And the women who wield power in the war, Margaret Thatcher and Jeane Kirkpatrick, could hardly be mistaken for feminists. Nevertheless, although the new *Mail on Sunday* can describe Thatcher as 'a leader with the touch of Churchill' (2 May), a few days later the 'Femail' column devoted a whole page to 'Crisis Chic' and an analysis of her wardrobe, which 'radiates steely resolve.' (4 May). The ideological war is carried on on all fronts.

Thus, even when the reporting in the popular press is partial, garbled and inconsistent, these newspapers continue to offer their readers a highly coherent ideological framework within which to interpret and make sense of the news.

Daily Star 6 April 1982.

Statistical tables

Table 1

The Falklands Population in the Census Years 1851-1980

Year	Population
1851	287[1]
1861	541[1]
1871	811[1]
1881	1,510
1891	1,789
1901	2,043
1911	2,272
1921	2,094
1931	2,392
1946	2,239
1953	2,230
1962	2,172
1972	1,957
1980	1,813[2]

1. Estimated.
2. This figure excludes 42 Royal Marines at Moody Brook Barracks and the crews and passengers of two visiting ships in Stanley Harbour on the Census Day.

Source: Falkland Islands Government, *Report of the Census*, 1980.

Table 2

British Aid to Argentina, 1976 to 1980

£000s	1976	1977	1978	1979	1980
Technical Cooperation	61	24	15	5	30
Financial Aid	—	—	—	—	—
Total	61	24	15	5	30

Students and Trainees financed under the Aid Programme

	Students	Trainees	Total
1980	24	39	63

Source: Overseas Development Administration, *British Aid Statistics*, 1976 to 1980.

127

Table 3

British Aid to the Falklands/Malvinas, 1976 to 1980

£000s	1976	1977	1978	1979	1980
Technical Cooperation	261	357	355	473	427
Financial Aid	1,233	758	1,765	442	587
Total	1,494	1,115	2,120	915	1,014

Students and Trainees financed under the Aid Programme

	Students	Trainees	Total
1980	5	11	16

Source: Overseas Development Administration, *British Aid Statistics*, 1976 to 1980.

Table 4

Foreign Investment in Argentina by Country of Origin (1977 to 1981)

United States of America	43.5%
Italy	14.3%
France	9.6%
Holland	9.2%
West Germany	6.4%
Switzerland	4.4%
Brazil	1.4%
Canada	1.3%
Japan	1.2%
Sweden	1.2%
Britain	0.8%

Source: Argentina, Ministry of Economy, *Weekly Economic Bulletin*, 9 November 1981.

Table 5

UK Trade with the Falklands/Malvinas 1980

SITC[1] Section	Imports from FI/Malvinas Value (£000s)	%	Exports to FI/Malvinas Value (£000s)	%
0. Food and live animals	5	0.2	258	12.4
1. Beverages and Tobacco	—	—	206	9.9
2. Crude Materials	2,787	97.9	36	1.7
3. Mineral Fuels and Lubricants	—	—	30	1.4
4. Animal and Vegetable Oils	—	—	5	0.2
5. Chemicals etc.	—	—	75	3.6
6. Manufactured Goods	21	0.7	275	13.2
7. Machinery and Transport	10	0.4	534	25.7
8. Miscellaneous Manufactures	7	0.2	215	10.3
9. Other Goods	17	0.6	448	21.5
Total	2,847	100.0	2,082	100.0

1. SITC: Standard international trade classification.
—: negligible.

Source: Overseas Trade Statistics of the United Kingdom 1980, Table II and V.

Table 6

UK Trade with Argentina 1980

SITC[1] Section	Imports from Argentina Value (£000s)	%	Exports to Argentina Value (£000s)	%
0. Food and Live animals	58,463	51.2	2,374	1.4
1. Beverages and Tobacco	1,193	1.0	7,603	4.4
2. Crude Materials	28,038	24.5	793	0.5
3. Mineral Fuels and Lubricants	—	—	413	0.2
4. Animal and Vegetable Oils	2,716	2.4	161	0.1
5. Chemicals etc.	5,757	5.0	22.463	13.0
6. Manufactured Goods	8,389	7.3	23,619	13.7
7. Machinery and Transport	7,291	6.4	96,081	55.6
8. Miscellaneous Manufactures	2,274	2.0	16,479	9.5
9. Other	165	0.1	2,844	1.6
Total	114,286	100.0	172,830	100.0

1. SITC: Standard international trade classification.
—: negligible.

Source: Overseas Trade Statistics of the United Kingdom 1980, Table II and V.

129

Table 7

Argentine Trade by Principal Country of Origin and Destination (1978)

Country of origin	Proportion of total imports	Destination Country	Proportion of total exports
EEC (9)	31%	EEC (9)	34%
USA	19%	Netherlands	10%
Germany (Fed. Rep)	12%	Brazil	9%
Brazil	9%	USA	9%
Italy	8%	Italy	8%
Japan	7%	USSR	6%
Chile	5%	Japan	6%
United Kingdom	4%	Germany (Fed. Rep.)	6%
France	4%	Spain	5%
Gabon	3%	Chile	3%
Spain	3%	United Kingdom	3%
Bolivia	3%	France	3%
Switzerland	2%	Venezuela	2%

Source: UN *1979 Yearbook of International Trade Statistics.* Vol.1, p.83.

Table 8

UK Sales of Major Weapons Systems to Argentina

No.	Designation	Description	Ordered	Delivered	No.	Comments
1		ACC	...	...	1	'Colossus': second hand
6		CMS	...	...	6	Second hand
2	Type 42	Destroyer	1970	1977/80	2	'Hercules' and 'Santissima Trinidad'. One built under licence in Argentina; one built in the UK
...	Seacat	ShAM	1970	1977/80	...	Supplied by Short Bros. Ltd, Belfast
44	Sea Dart Mk. 1	ShAM	1970	1977/80	44	Made by British Aerospace
20	Tigercat	SAM	1968/1981	...	...	10 for the army and 10 for the marines. Made by Short Bros. Ltd, Belfast
...	Blowpipe	Portable SAM	1981	...	...	
10	Lynx	ASW hel	1977/79	1979/81	(6)	Made by Westland Aircraft Ltd for ASW duty on Argentine ships
...	Shorland	AC	...	...	...	For gendarmerie. Made by Short Bros. Ltd, Belfast
9	Canberra B62	Bomber	...	...	...	Ordered early 1970s

... information not available.
( ) uncertain. SIPRI estimates.
(See table on page xx for list of abbreviations).

Sources: Stockholm International Peace Research Institute, *World Armaments and Disarmament, SIPRI Yearbook 1981*, Taylor and Francis, London, 1981, Appendix 7A.
SIPRI Press release, *Arms sales to Argentina*, SIPRI, Stockholm, 1982.
Campaign Against the Arms Trade, *Factsheet 32: British Military Involvement in Argentina* (Updated version), CAAT, London, 1982.

Table 9

UK Military Equipment Sales (Non-Major Weapons Systems) to Argentina

No.	Description	Ordered	Supplied	No.	Comments
100	Sub-machine guns	...	1975	100	Sterling Armament Co. 5 supplied with silencers
...	'Isis' sights for Skyhawk Aircraft	...	1976	...	Made by Ferranti
...	'Seaspray' radar for Lynx Hel	...	1977	...	Made in Edinburgh by Ferranti
...	'Clearscan' radar for FPB	...	1979	...	Made by Decca, Walton-on-Thames
...	HF and VHF radios for coastal PB	...	1979	...	
...	Gear pumps for German supplied destroyers	1980	...	...	Vickers, Barrow-in-Furness
...	Radio transmitters for naval stations	1981	...	...	Redifussion, Surbiton
...	Aero engines	...	...	...	Made by Rolls-Royce. Delivery uncertain but some reported sighted in 1981
...	'Morgrip' bolts for naval propellors	1981	...	...	Made by Doncasters Moorside
...	ESM	1981	...	...	Made by Racal-Decca for eavesdropping on radio and radar systems
250	Mach/airspeed indicators for Pucará counter-insurgency aircraft	1981	...	...	Made by Smiths Indudstries
...	Pneumatic controls for PB and Corvettes	1981	...	...	Vosper Thorneycroft
...	Modification for Type 42 destroyers	...	...	...	Work done in late 1970s by Plessey and Ferranti

... information not available.
(See table on page xx for list of abbreviations).

Source: Campaign Against the Arms Trade, *Factsheet 32: British Military Involvement in Argentina* (Updated version), CAAT, London, 1982.

Table 10

Selected List of Major Weapons Systems Procured by Argentina, 1977-1981

Supplier	No.	Designation	Description	Ordered	Delivered	No.
Austria	57	Cuirassier	LT/TD	1981	1981	57
Belgium	...	BDX	APC	(1979)	1980	13
France	3	A-69 Class	Frigate	1978/79	1978/81	3
	7	Mirage-3	Fighter	1978	1980	7
	14	Super Etendard	Naval fighter/bomber	1979	1981	(6)
	...	AMX-13	LT	1969	1970-78[1]	...
	36	ERC-90 Lynx	AC	1979	...	...
	60	ERC-90S Sagaie	AC	1981	...	...
	...	VAB	APC	(1981)	1981	2
	...	MM-38 Exocet	ShShM	1970/79	1977/81	...
	24	Otomat-2	ShShM	1979	...	...
	1,000	HOT	ATM	1980	...	...
	(80)	Roland-1	Landmobile SAM	1981	...	...
Israel	2	Dubur Class	Coastal PB	1977	1978	2
	26	Dagger	Fighter/strike	1978	1980	26
	16	Dagger	Fighter/strike	1981	1981[2]	16
Italy	10	MB-339A	Jet trainer	(1980)	(1981)[3]	(10)
	48	Apside/Albatross	ShAM	(1979)	...	...
Netherlands	8	F-27/28	Transport	1976/80	1977/81	8
Spain	5	B-119	Corvette	1979	...	
Sweden	50	RBS-53 Bantam	ATM	1975	1977	(50)
Switzerland	...	Roland	APC	1969	1973/79[1]	...
USA	40	A-4 Skyhawk	Fighter/strike	1975/76	1977/78	40
	2	Learjet-35A	Transport/Recce	1976	1978	2
	1	Learjet-35A	Transport/Recce	1980	1981	1
	5	CH-47C Chinook	Hel	1977/78	1979/80	5
	4	S-2E Tracker	Maritime PB	1977	1978	4
	2	KC-130H	Tanker	1978	1980	2
West Germany	4	Meko-360	Destroyer	1979	...	...
	6	Meko-140	Corvette	1979	...	...
	2	Type 1400	Submarine	1977	...	...
	4	Type 1700	Submarine	1977	...	...
	20		FPB	1977	1979/81	(3)
	...	TAM	MT	1976	1980/81	225

1 Produced under licence   3 Unconfirmed   ( ) uncertain, SIPRI estimates
2 Second batch reportedly delivered   ... information not available

Sources: Stockholm International Peace Research Institute, *Arms Sales to Argentina* (Press Release), SIPRI, Stockholm, 1982. pp.5-10. SIPRI, *World Armaments and Disarmament*, SIPRI Yearbook 1981, Taylor and Francis, London, 1981, Appendix 7A.

Abbreviations

		CMS	Coastal Minesweeper	PB	Patrol Boat
AC	Armoured Car	ESM	Electronic support measures	SAM	Surface-to-air Missile
ACC	Aircraft Carrier	FPB	Fast Patrol Boat	ShAM	Ship-to-air Missile
APC	Armoured Personnel Carrier	Hel	Helicopter	ShShM	Ship-to-Ship Missile
ASW	Anti-submarine Warfare	LT	Light Tank	TD	Tank Destroyer
ATM	Anti-tank Missile	MT	Medium Tank		

135